JUST A LITTLE MORE

Sister Giles

Grosvenor House
Publishing Limited

This book is published by
Grosvenor House Publishing Ltd
28-30 High Street, Guildford, Surrey, GU1 3EL.
www.grosvenorhousepublishing.co.uk

A CIP record for this book
is available from the British Library

ISBN 978-1-78148-855-3

Just a little more
And we shall see the almond tree in blossom
The marbles shining in the sun
The sea, the curling waves.
Just a little more
Let us rise just a little higher.

George Seferis (trans. Rex Warner)

A few weeks ago I was invited to a small party. The day was frosty and the mulled wine was a complement to the logs burning in the old fireplace. I found myself beside someone I had not met. "I remember you well!" she smiled. I was disconcerted, trying to recall any particular misdemeanour so memorable. "I attended an address you gave several years ago," she explained, "and something you said has always remained with me -"

Astonished, I could not recall the particular occasion.

"I suppose you have no record of your talks?" she asked. She sounded quite serious.

As it happens, I always have retained copies of retreat days or talks. I am fearful of repeating myself. My unrecognised friend urged me to bring them together. Home again, I unearthed the file in the spare-room cupboard. The notes were held together by paper-clips and some had rusted, marking the thin paper. The typing had left a lot to be desired. I do not own a computer. Now I have sorted them into a semblance of order, collating the pages into sections. Perhaps I have been over-persuaded. I can easily blame my unrecognised friend. On the other hand, who am I, for whom 'obedience' in my enclosed community was ever a precept, not to make at least an attempt at answering a request?

This, for what it is worth, is what I have tried to do.

And I know that a great debt of gratitude is due to Rob Pedzinski and Cornelia Dichio for their help in the presenting of the typescript.

Address for the Week of Christian Unity

How happy I am to be with you today - for not only is it January 25, which the Church keeps as the Conversion of St Paul, but it is also the day on which I took my first vows as a religious sister. And the 'motto' I took that day came from the lovely seventeenth chapter of St John, where Our Lord prays '*May they all be one*'.

That prayer of Christ is surely reflected in the response made by many in this week of Christian unity. Of course there are differences, not always easy to forget in our varying traditions of faith, but I believe there ARE areas in which we can indeed be united, and I think in particular of the specific areas of prayer, and of the love that should mark us out as Christian.

The same St John, in his first Letter, wrote: 'Dear friends, let us love one another because love comes from God...and God showed his love for us by sending his only Son into the world, so that we might have life through him.' And St Paul in his Letter to the Ephesians wrote much the same thing: 'Because of his Love, God had already decided that through Jesus Christ, he would make US his sons...'

I have a small book - some of you may know it - by the Abbé de Tourville. It contains his letters of direction written in the last century, and I have often quoted from his words on God's love for us. He writes: 'Be absolutely certain that God loves you, devotedly and individually: loves you as you are. How often this conviction is lacking even in those souls who are most devoted to God! They make repeated efforts to love him, they experience the joy of loving, and yet how little they know, how little they realise, that God loves them incomparably more than they will ever know how to love Him. Think only of this and say to yourself 'I am loved by God more than I can either conceive or understand.' Let this fill all your soul and all your prayer and never leave you. You will soon see that this is the way to find God. It contains the whole of St John's teaching: 'As for us, we have believed in the love which God has for us.'... Accustom yourself to the wonderful thought that God loves you with a tenderness, a generosity, and an intimacy which surpasses all your dreams.'

Having spent nearly twenty-five years in an enclosed community, I have come to see the sometimes amazing results of answered prayer. How many requests we had for our prayers: those who were ill, the bereaved, the lonely, to name but a few. And it wasn't because we spent long hours on our knees (we did, but that was simply because of the daily pattern) it was, I am sure, because we had dedicated ourselves to God's Love that enabled us, so to speak, to be what I used to imagine a *hosepipe* for his love - and by the same token for his healing.

And I am certain that this 'hosepipe' business is applicable to us all. You don't have to be dressed in a long brown habit with a rope round your middle, go barefoot (as we did!) and visit the chapel six times a day. *All of us*, as Christians, have a commitment to Christ and the certainty of his love (we were made members of his family at our baptism) and it is important that we *maintain* this channel for the love he has bequeathed us. And I suppose the thing that most activates the 'hosepipe' is the *unblocking* of it so that his love may flow through us freely to others. (That is when the miracles occur!) Jesus said to his disciples 'I have told you this that your joy may be complete', and he went on 'My commandment is that you love one another, just as I have loved you.' Isn't it the impedimenta of self-righteousness, uncharity and - sometimes, I think - the sheer lack of humility with which we clog up the flow?

If we take time, and perhaps this week is as good as any, to realise in our quiet prayer the certainty of Our Lord's presence within us, then we shall almost automatically open ourselves to the love of God 'which is an inflowing and an outpouring tide' as the philosopher Ruysbroek once wrote. (We are back to the 'hosepipe' again!) St Paul, in his Letter to the Colossians, told them: 'and the secret is that Christ is IN you, which means that you will share in the glory of God. So we preach God to everyone, and with all possible wisdom we warn and teach them in order to bring each one into God's presence as a mature individual in *union with Christ.*'

Once we have caught a glimpse of what that indwelling of Christ can mean for us, we can also understand that his presence is never restricted to one individual rather than another. Any 'restricting' is on our part, inasmuch as we are indifferent. Could we but perceive this, how few antagonisms would remain!

From an address to
the Churches' Fellowship

When I first entered the Order, all I knew was that in doing so I was obeying an insistent call within me to 'give myself' in this way. It seemed totally unreasonable. (I actually remember saying to my mother in a moment of dramatic realisation "Well I suppose it's no worse than imprisonment for life!") but I knew that, somehow, for me, the thing had to be done.

At first, as a novice, one is tossed into a world where customs seem strange. On my first evening we were given kippers for supper. Delicious. But with furtive glances at my silent neighbour, I noticed these were being eaten with a teaspoon. How strange. "Ah, well," I thought, "teaspoon it is!" - and I subsequently gathered supper was *always* eaten with a teaspoon, a bone teaspoon, which was a tradition from much earlier times.

What are teaspoons and silence to do with God, one asks? Well I am sure God can get along quite easily without any help from us, quaint tradition or otherwise - but then it isn't God, of course, but WE who have to do the getting on. One may question the teaspoons, but if it is part of a way of discipline that frees one to learn and listen and become open to God - then even a kipper has its place!

In fact this is just one of the things one does learn: that everything has its place. It may come in an instant, it may take twenty years, but the realisation of what it means to be part of God's creation, made by Him, upheld by Him and loved by Him, whoever we are and wherever we are, is at once humbling and healing and a source of extraordinary happiness. Then, I think, the sense of 'oneness in Christ' quoted so frequently by St Paul, takes on a new reality. One gradually senses the 'oneness' with those for whom one meets or prays. And how authentic this becomes once we pray particularly for someone. Do we not find ourselves coming to 'know' them in a way we scarcely guessed before? I have been astonished over the years at the sense of 'awareness' I have had of those for whom I have prayed or been asked to pray.

This is not really surprising. God is *love*! And I suppose if we desire to become 'his Love', to let Him speak and act through us, then we shall gradually find ourselves loving the world, with however faint a resemblance, in *His* way. "Not I, but Christ working within me," as St Paul wrote. Is not this the way of a Christian believer? A way of simplicity and trust; and of turning to that ineffable power within us with childlike faith?

From an address to the Worthing School of Prayer

In an address on the occasion of one of my community's profession - the day when a nun pronounces her vows – I remember the visiting priest underlining the fact that by her profession she was making space for God. The dictionary definition of 'space' is 'an interval between two points', and I suppose we could say that the two points in this case were our lives - and God. Today, I think we could say that we are particularly trying to fill (or perhaps I mean empty) that space - to fill it with the conscious sense of God's presence and to empty it of some of the accumulated clutter that inevitably besets our daily living.

Somewhere along the line we have to learn how to find that 'presence' within. It *is* there, even if we are often unaware of the fact. When the Holy Spirit came down on the Apostles- and through them to us - He came to *dwell in our hearts*, no less. When you come to think of it, to realise within yourself that the Holy Spirit is there in your heart with all his gifts, it makes you stop in your tracks! It is so easy to procrastinate, to put off that moment of quiet when we can 'Be still and know that I am God' as the psalms admonish us in another verse. Being still is one of the great inabilities of our time. Always we tend to say 'Oh, I'll just finish here, then I can relax with nothing on my mind-' and, of course we never *do* feel relaxed or free, and the moment of quiet recedes like a mirage, always just out of reach.

I should like to quote a passage from Archbishop Anthony Bloom's *Courage to Pray*. Some of you may already know it, but I should like to share it with you because I think it illustrates what I mean about finding that presence of God within oneself.

'A very old woman came to me. She told me that she had constantly recited the prayer of Jesus for many years, but she had never been given the experience of the presence of God. Young as I was, I found a simple answer to her problem. "How can God get a word in edgeways if you never stop talking? Give him a chance. Keep quiet." "How can I do that?" she said. I then gave her some advice that I have since given to others because it worked on that occasion. I advised her after breakfast to tidy her room and make it as pleasant as possible and sit down in a position where she could see the whole room, the window on to the garden, the icons with their little oil lamps. "When you have sat down, rest for a quarter of an hour in the presence of God, but take care not to pray. Be as quiet as you can and as you obviously can't do nothing, knit before the Lord and tell me what happens." After a few days she came back happily. She had felt the presence of God. I asked her curiously what had happened. She said she had done exactly what I had suggested. She sat down and. looked about her quietly and peacefully feeling she had the right to be inactive and not praying and for the first time for years, she said, she noticed that the room was peaceful and pleasant to be in. She looked at it and saw it for the first time. There was an encounter between her and the place she had lived in for many years without ever seeing. Then she became aware of the peace and silence around her, a peace and silence accentuated by the ticking of her clock and the clicking of her needles on the arms of her chair. Gradually this silence which had been outside her came within her and enveloped her. The silence took her out of herself into a richer silence which was not just the absence of noise but rich in itself, and in its centre she found a presence. And when she felt this presence she was moved to pray, but from the depth of this silence, not in floods of words and a whirl of thoughts, but gently and quietly taking each word from the silence and offering it to God. Of its own accord her prayer had become the expression of her inner silence and part of the silence of God which she had felt.'

This day, made up of so many moments, *is* God's gift to us. Each day of our lives is his gift to us because he created us, holds us in being and *dwells within us*. Without him we would not exist! This day - each day - can bring times of difficulty, anxiety or anguish of some kind or another. We can be hurt by unkindness, or the forgetfulness of others, we can be strained by overwork or the 'heats and burdens of the day', and in none of this can we be expected to find joy or a cause for rejoicing. But *step on the brake*! Stop for a second, try to centre ourselves and get a sight of God's will in all this! In the midst of even the greatest trials we can mentally 'push the button' that gives us strength and courage and humour. We *have* that means once we remember that He is there. And as we come to practice that 'presence of God' we shall discover that it *is* possible to say 'yes' in our hearts to whatever is being asked. We shall recognise God's providence and, however hard at first, we shall somehow find ourselves with inward peace. It was Dante, that great poet, who wrote '*in His will, our peace*'.

And, after a little, we shan't even have to knit!

THOUGHT FOR THE DAY –
BBC Radio Sussex

I attended a funeral last week. Everyone had their own sadness and sense of loss to bear, and the service took its course with all the customary care and solemnity. There were hymns, and a loving tribute from the pulpit and the flowers laid on the ground outside were a mass of colour. We gathered there afterwards, comforting and comforted.

I remember watching at the bedside of a sister in my community several years ago. She was ninety-nine and nearing the end of her journey. Scarcely conscious, all at once she somehow raised herself from her pillows and with a truly radiant smile cried "Wait for me! I'm coming, I'm coming" - Very shortly after that she died, and the smile still seemed to be there.

I suppose it is really the uncertainty of the whole thing that frightens us. Perhaps it must be something like that for a baby about to be born - how warm and secure it has been for nine months, cradled within the womb! I'm sure any sort of 'shedding' of the familiar will clutch at the heart. Yet isn't it only the chrysalis of ourselves we leave behind in dying? Doesn't the reality lie in the release of the spirit, free and unfettered, in preparation for unimaginable joy?

Do you remember those lines from Francis Thompson's poem, *The Hound of Heaven*? Towards the end he writes:

All that thy child's mistake
Fancies as lost, I have stored for thee at home:
Rise, clasp my hand, and come.

I have thought of that lately, and especially at last week's family grief.

Morning Address at
Arundel Parish Eucharist

When the Vicar asked me to share some thoughts on 'prayer' with you, I felt there could be no more appropriate time at which to begin - for we are here this morning at this celebration of the Eucharist, the heart of Christian faith.

As a Roman Catholic, I cannot at this time receive communion with you, but I can indeed be united in faith and it is in this faith, it seems to me, that all prayer has its source.

It is the most precious gift we have, for it leads us to a supernatural form of life. To increase this supernatural form of life, we pray. Prayer could be described as the fertiliser, so to speak, that brings the plant on. We *need* to pray in order to grow.

And the point of the whole thing is to unite oneself to God's will for us, to be open, as a flower to the sun, to the extent that we begin to get a faint perception of our unique place in creation. God created us, knows us, holds us in being, and loves us.

I think this matter of his loving us is something we tend to forget. To help become aware of it, we need to be still a moment - 'be still and know that I am God', the psalmist wrote - and we need to silence the tumult of our thoughts and impulses and so on, in order to become aware of God's presence. This also puts the thing in the right perspective, because it is an acknowledgement of our smallness, our createdness, before God.

So we can say that prayer makes us more aware and gives us confidence. 'We of ourselves can do nothing,' but - as St Paul went on to say - 'I can do all things *through Christ* which strengtheneth me.' The more we pray the better it goes. The Benedictine abbot who wrote those words also used to say 'Pray as you *can* and not as you can't' - a very wise counsel!

Usually when we first come to pray we are conscious of the ninety-nine important matters slicing through our busy minds or, if we manage to remain composed, drop off to sleep! But what really matters is that we have actually set aside even the smallest amount of time, regularly, and that we stay put even when we continue the shopping list with the surface of our minds - or drop off. We have given that time to God, *in our will*, which is what matters. If we persevere, sooner or later, we shall more easily remain still, our thoughts quietened, and in the silence we shall more readily hear God's word. I don't mean we shall necessarily hear it like Samuel, who kept getting up because he thought old Eli was calling, but in the way that we find ourselves saying 'Speak Lord, for thy servant is listening.' And as we become adapted to this way of listening, I think we shall begin to realise the sense of God's presence. It *is* there, with us always, but we tend to make so much noise that we let it go.

You remember the lay brother, Brother Lawrence, working in his monastery kitchen: he became so practiced in this awareness that his interior conversation with God was continual, in all the seemingly unimportant little things of the day. So it can be with us - and a source of continual joy. Whatever the circumstances of our lives, nothing need separate us from God.

Today, gathered here, God's love for each of us is accentuated at this service, and later I should like to expand on these thoughts. In the meantime, who but St Paul could write so succinctly: "Then what can separate us from the love of Christ?...For I am convinced that there is nothing in death or life, in the realms of the spirit or superhuman powers, in the world as it is or the world as it shall be, in the forces of the universe, in heights or depths - nothing in all creation that can separate us from the love of God in Christ Jesus Our Lord."

THOUGHT FOR THE DAY –
BBC Radio Sussex

Last week I stayed for a few days in Edinburgh. It was a lovely break, and I love that Scottish city. I was taken to a concert in the Usher Hall, walked down Prince's Street pressing my nose against shop windows and, on another day, explored the old part of the city, climbing steps and steep hills and inspecting passageways and courtyards where history seemed tangible. I was exhilarated.

One evening, watching the sunset unfold great scarlet banners as I stood riveted at the window of the top floor flat, I suddenly spotted two herons flapping overhead. They were making their way towards the distant playing fields. I could hardly believe my eyes. Herons in Edinburgh!

Down here in Sussex, I see the old heron beating his way along the river on his routine course and think nothing of it, but that pair flying over the tall grey houses of Edinburgh really surprised and delighted me. "Hi!" I shouted, as if they could hear. Against that sunset they seemed immeasurably lovely.

Isn't it silly how much we take things for granted and only when seen out of context does the shape or colour of beauty become relevant. All those everyday things, like cauliflowers - we never think about them. Yet when we took a holiday in France how enchanted we were at the local market, vegetables piled high and served to us by stallholders with brown weathered faces, and a distinctly French smell permeating the little town.

I suppose gradually learning to 'see' is what it's all about. As the poet Gerard Manley Hopkins wrote:

"There lives the dearest freshness deep down things -"

And so there does, if only we could train ourselves to look for it.

THOUGHT FOR THE DAY –
BBC Radio Sussex

I visited North Devon in August. I set off at 5am to avoid the worst of the traffic and reached the rocky cove without difficulty.

As always, the impact of the high headland lifted my heart. But I was not on holiday. I'd come to see an elderly friend who'd had a massive stroke two years ago. She'd been enormously active always and finding herself suddenly paralysed down one side, could scarcely believe it. Sheer determination brought her through the months and months of work on her muscles and limbs. Now she could take a few steps with a metal crutch for support.

It was lovely to see her so much better and, later, I offered to push her down to the sea wall in what she called her "wheelbarrow" - the padded chrome chair she had from the Red Cross.

We bumped our way down the uneven lane till we reached the wall where, in winter, the sea pounded the little jetty. This evening the tide was out. We saw children playing in the sand and clambering over the rocks. We knew what they would find in the little rock pools - the sea anemones, the tiny fronds of pink seaweed, the sudden scurrying of shrimp or crab.

There was no question of getting the wheeled chair down, but we could share it in our memories. We *knew* what it was like. We watched two cormorants fly low over the sea and we waved to a couple of children picking their way gingerly over the great slabs with shrimping nets in their hands.

After a while we turned for home again, my old friend sighing with contentment. I tried to think of myself in her place, tied down and prevented from doing anything just as and when I wished; imprisoned by my body. I should have been a dreadful patient.

"Two men looked out from prison bars,
The one saw mud, the other stars..."

I knew which of them described my elderly friend.

From a Quiet Day at North Stoke

What a lovely time to meet - Easter so recent, and the Ascension and Pentecost so soon to come! I thought we might think for a moment of those disciples who walked with Jesus, not recognising him, on the road to Emmaus. There they were, telling him of the horrifying events of the past week that culminated in the crucifixion - the crucifixion of him whom they had considered their Messiah. "Have you not *heard*?" they asked, incredulous. And not until they stopped to eat and they saw Jesus break the bread, did the 'scales fall from their eyes.'

Is it not sometimes like this for us? We cruise along busily, so intent on this or that, never stopping except to check our watches. Suddenly some unexpected event, perhaps of great joy, perhaps on the other hand of great pain, has the effect of opening our eyes to a deeper meaning.

We see this in times of national disaster. Unspeakable grief, and then in the aftermath of bereavement something else comes to light: a sense of unity, or immense charity far exceeding normal practice.

Where is God in this?

The fact is that God is always with us, unrecognised or not. We were each created in his love. He is our Father in heaven. We have every right to turn to him in our needs.

A year or two ago, the mother of my young godson asked if I would explain God to him. A tall order! We were all walking through the field together, searching for caterpillars. Christopher particularly wanted to find those orange and black striped sort, the caterpillars one finds massed round the stems of coltsfoot wildflowers so prolific up here. Actually it was the wrong season and we searched in vain, so we walked on towards the river, where we had a successful game of 'Poohsticks' standing on the bridge. When it began to rain we decided to take refuge in the little downland church nearby, passing several grazing sheep obligingly adding excitement as we made our way to the porch.

Once inside, I asked Christopher if he knew about churches. He looked blank - he was only five - so I explained that we could always come to church to say 'thank you' to God (and sometimes to sing to him too.) "Did you know about God?" I asked. Before he could think up an answer, I explained how God loved us all and how, for instance, he particularly wanted Christopher to be born because he loved him so much. I suggested that God asked his mother and father to help in the making of Christopher and - because they too wanted him so much - how they gladly said yes. Churches were lovely places to come and say thank you, or to talk to God 'inside', but we could always stop and talk to God *anywhere*, especially if we were worried or frightened. He seemed satisfied with that and when we emerged the rain had stopped - and we found a tiny snail on the way home, albeit no caterpillars.

From a Quiet Day at Berrington

The Christian Dictionary tells us that in the first three centuries the period of fasting before Easter did not normally exceed two or three days. The first mention of a period of forty days dates from AD 325.

Perhaps we were observing the older liturgy in my convent. We had met in 'Chapter' just before Ash Wednesday to discuss the possibility of eating our old hens in the interests of economy. Never eating meat, this was a controversial subject. Some of the older members of the community felt it the thin end of the wedge. Being democratic, we decided to pray about the matter, and to meet the following week to take a vote. On the Thursday, a van drew up and to the amazement of the sister on the door two men alighted. They carried a butcher's tray on which were displayed seven dressed chickens, several pounds of pork sausages and a separate bowl of prepared chipped potatoes in water. They had come, they explained, from a film location at a nearby village. Lunch had been cancelled owing to the indisposition of the leading lady, and they thought we might be glad of a free lunch.

We took this as a sign from the Lord!

The older members of the community, ever obedient to such obvious indications, withdrew their objections and we sat down to roast chicken, sausages and chips on the first Friday of Lent!

Lent is a preparation for EASTER. We deny ourselves in commemoration of Christ's forty days in the wilderness, and to bear witness to the fact that we are Christian.

Christians believe in the resurrection. Christ's resurrection from the dead is the centre of Christianity. The light from the

Paschal Mystery permeates the entire liturgical year. We believe, with St John, that Christ came that we might have life everlasting.

We receive the new life in Christ at our baptism. It is renewed and strengthened by the sacraments each time we receive them. Hippolytus, writing in the second century, has some lovely words about this light and life of Christ:

'Life extends over all beings and fills them
with unlimited light; he who was 'before the
daystar' and before the heavenly bodies, immortal
and vast, the great Christ, shines over all
beings more brightly than the sun. Therefore
a day of long, eternal light is ushered in for
us who believe in him, a day which is never blotted
out: the mystical Passover.'

When we think of 'going to church', that weekly visit to our local parish, with perhaps the irreverent hope that the sermon will not be too long, or the fear that the Yorkshire puddings will be late into the oven, we have rather forgotten the immensity of the Mystical Passover. Those early Fathers reverberated with the joy of the resurrection.

Perhaps a 'day of quiet' is a time when we can let go for a few hours, untether ourselves from the complexities of everyday life, as we have made it. We do need to 'be still', to make the conscious effort to be so, in order to silence the outer clamour. Those of you who practice any form of meditation will know this. 'Be still and know that I am God' as the psalmist wrote, really is the key to un-lock that inner door. It is amazing how much the awareness of the central core of God's love within each of us can grow in this way.

I once used the analogy of a 'kipper' to demonstrate this: Consider yourself a kipper, open down the middle, the bones all there, about to go under the grill. Let the light and love of God 'cook' you. Ask him to reach all those bony bits, all the crevices you have forgotten about. Relax, dispose yourself to this all-pervading light.'

Once perceived in yourself, of course, it is easier to recognise him in others. 'Christ *in* you', wrote St Paul to the Colossians. That is when compassion grows: you are able to put yourself in another's place. I remember my novice mistress saying 'Forget self, and you will become a saint.' It is very hard indeed to forget self. Anyone with teenage children will know that. "You *forget* yourself!" I remember being scolded in reprimand. Actually, of course, it was not myself, but everyone else I was forgetting.

I was sent a booklet about an old lady in Canada some time ago. Bedridden and in her eighties, she suddenly found a purpose in life by praying for the men she saw from her window. They were working on a construction site. Each day she thought of them as she watched from her bed, praying for their safety as they perched high on scaffolding or roof ridge. After a while someone told the men of the old lady's vigil and they went to thank her, telling her of their progress, filling her in with all their doings. They even presented her with one of their red hard-hats. It was only after their work had been completed that the old lady peacefully died. Her 'forgetfulness of self' had spread far beyond her small room. Nor is it necessary to have good health. Many are the times I have asked infirm or elderly friends to pray for me. Their support has been tangible.

You see, prayer *transforms*. By prefacing each mundane thing we undertake with the prayer that it be done 'in his name' - or in whatever way the Holy Spirit inspires us to dedicate the action - we are placing it 'on automatic', so to speak. It becomes something 'given' to God, and then used in his eternal plan. (Nice to think that shopping in Sainsbury or cleaning one's teeth is part of the eternal plan.) Yet this is what life is about. We gradually come to see that everything is in him and he is in us. As we practice prayer, and it may take many years, our sense of God's presence becomes simple. We can begin to see his hand in everything, even adversity, which he allows to strengthen us.

From an address for
Barrow Hills Prize Day

When Mr Connolly asked me to come here today, I tried to decline the invitation, because I thought you should have a film star, or someone glamorous (like Britney Spears). But he was most persistent, so I found it difficult to refuse. And there is another reason why I really should not be handing you prizes: when I was at *my* prep school, in the days when maths was called arithmetic, I only achieved 3/100 in that subject - which goes to show something, though I'm not sure what.

But it is lovely to be with you this evening, and to have been taken round the school the other week. I can see what a particularly happy school it is. I loved my own prep school and always said that I learned more there than I ever did later. And I think one of the main things I learned was about 'friendship', and the sharing of all those things that go to shape our lives when we grow up.

You have been told that I am a sister, and I should just like to tell you that it was in Italy, on a visit to Assisi where St Francis lived, and his friend St Clare - who founded my order of nuns eight hundred years ago (though I am not as old as *that*) when I knew I wanted to follow God in that way. I'm sure you will know about St Francis and his love for every creature. All the birds used to flock round him, and he would talk to them, telling them how God loved them. I think of this when the tame blackbird comes to my bird table each morning.

And that message St Francis gave to the birds is the same message all the followers of St Francis and St Clare try to bring to everyone: that God *loves* them, wherever they are.

Today, some of you have won prizes and some of you have not. Of course it is lovely to win a prize, but it is not the end of the world if you have not. You see, God doesn't mind about prizes, he simply wants you to know that he loves you anyway.

As I told you, I only achieved 3/100 for maths, but I grew up to be very happy, and when I look back at my prep school I am enormously grateful for those days. I *thought* I should go on to be an actress, or to marry and have lots of children - but in the end God wanted me to follow St Francis, so you never know where your life will lead. But everything you learn here, at Barrow Hills, will help to prepare you for whatever lies ahead. And it will always be an adventure.

And now I am going to leave you with a simple ABC, and it is this: A - always be *Aware* that God loves you. B - always do your *Best* for others and C - go forward in *Courage*, because your guardian angel will always be there to lead the way. Happy holidays!

THOUGHT FOR THE DAY –
BBC Radio Sussex

My sister has just acquired a puppy. His name is Sam. He's a black working cocker spaniel and already his ears are lengthening and the 'feathers' on his legs are giving promise of entanglements to come.

She brought him up to me for his first walk the other day. We didn't take him far, but it was marvellous to see him investigate all the smells and intoxicating trails down the lane, his small tail wagging incessantly, his eyes bright. Everything was new and exciting. Even the cabbage-white butterflies he disturbed in the field seemed to fly ahead of him for his special delight. We laughed at his lively enthusiasm.

Isn't it sad how dulled at the edges those early bright days of our own can become in later life? We are wiser now, and we don't have so many new things to experience - or perhaps we crave for them and discover emptiness where we had imagined stimulating satisfaction. The butterflies we chase are not so carefree.

Yet - don't you sometimes catch a glimpse of regained joy at special moments? A brand-new summer morning, perhaps, with everything shining and uncluttered - or the first sliver of a new moon as the evening sky fades to shell blue?

I believe these moments of natural loveliness will always have power to remind us of a more profound remembered joy. I think it was Evelyn Underhill who wrote: 'I come in the little things, saith the Lord' - and watching that puppy bound through the long sweet grass, I thought I could see what she meant.

THOUGHT FOR THE DAY –
BBC Radio Sussex

The friend I stayed with in North Wales the other week took me for a long walk into the hills. We climbed past fields edged with dry-stone walls (there were clumps of thyme and harebells patterned beside the path) and the steep track revealed ever more breathtaking views as we reached the crest of our particular summit. We were only in the foothills of the actual mountains, but we could see them all round, silent and towering with their recognisable contours and the distant Snowdon crowning the range to the north.

As we stood there, resting and marvelling, we spotted three buzzards high above, circling and weaving on great silent wings, their flight almost a dance as they crossed and re-crossed, swooped and sped down the long valley, the whole sky theirs. We felt so small on that vast hillside.

The following day, on my way home, I struggled off the train at Euston, pushed my way to the Underground, and the only climbing I did was up the escalator at Victoria. A far cry from Snowdon as I joined the throng of commuters endlessly making their way up and down those moving stairways.

And yet, I thought to myself, who knows what precious memories of their own might occupy the minds of those we pass so casually. I often think of that when I sit on trains or buses. Things are seldom what they seem.

'I carry you in my heart -' wrote the poet E. E. Cummings, 'anywhere I go, you go -'

Not unlike those wheeling buzzards with all the valley beneath them, we do have the freedom to carry innumerable treasures within our hearts, wherever we find ourselves.

THOUGHT FOR THE DAY –
BBC Radio Sussex

I always have a terrible time with tin-openers. I broke the one on the kitchen wall and can *never* manage the sort you clip on before turning a kind of screw as the point bites in to the top of the tin. As for those key things attached to the lid of sardine tins, I am incapable of rolling back the metal in the required direction- I once had to re-tile part of the kitchen when I inadvertently pulled out a large chunk of plaster by trying to open a tin too heavy for the fixture.

Yet I quite like gadgets and am always ready to investigate those belonging to friends. Actually I'm a sucker for those catalogues that come tucked into newspapers. Fortunately I haven't the means to purchase their advertised wares.

Yesterday it struck me how much we all depend on things that 'make life easier'. I suppose we are a gadget-conscious world! I don't suppose our ancestors were any less happy without them - and certainly their prevalence hasn't done much to provide food for the starving around the world, or to discourage the plight of refugees, or any of the other shattering agonies we hear about or see on our television screens.

Of course I am probably not making a valid comparison, but I am sure you will know what I mean. It does bring one up short sometimes when you realise that tins need to be opened to release their contents, and that the starving of the world still wait for rain. Have we, I sometimes wonder, slipped up on our priorities?

From a Quiet Day given at
The Hermitage

Yesterday we kept the feastday of St Clare. Having been an enclosed member of her Order for many years, I suppose you could say that I came under her influence. Before I entered the community, she had been for me a sort of 'double act' with St Francis - Brother Sun, Sister Moon, so to speak, like Zeffirelli's film. (I have to say that when this was shown to us on a small screen in the convent parlour, we were shamelessly reduced to giggles at the more sentimental bits.) Years of harvesting potatoes from our field, washing our chemises in stone troughs - like those photographs of St Therese of Lisieux in the 1890s - and other manual and menial tasks associated with a poverty-ruled penitential Order, somehow made short work of the more romantic aspects of our vocation. And in any case tiredness took its toll on romance.

Yet one came to love greatly the way of life St Clare advocated. Hers was a different 'love-story'. For she taught that in trying to learn the way of contemplative love, one need never be confined to the external enclosure of the convent. There need be no limit to the territory of loving, for the more consciously one loves, acknowledging God as the source of that love, the more deeply happy one can become. In the dedication of one's life to God, even when enclosed, it is possible to participate in the world's 'activity' because, in God, in his love, there is nowhere one cannot reach. "Be still and know that I am God", said the psalmist, and it is in this inner silence that the word of God's love becomes audible.

Taking a day of quiet, such as we have today, enables us to empty our minds of life's trivia for an hour or two, and allow space for that sense of God's love to infuse us. 'The love of God is an inflowing and an outpouring tide,' wrote Ruysbroek in the 13th century.

Of course not everyone can become - should become - an enclosed Poor Clare (or Carmelite or Benedictine or Cistercian) but we can, and do, all share in the pursuit of prayer. Some are attracted to a contemplative sort of prayer, content to wait on his love - others perhaps are called to a more 'active' kind. The method of prayer is really immaterial. What matters is our recognition of God's love, together with the Holy Spirit, which 'activates' the prayer. Needless to say we have all at times been like the small boy caught stealing ripe pears: as he clambered frantically over the orchard wall he was heard to mutter fervently "Holy Mary, Mother of God, pray for us sinners *now, now, now,* and at the hour of our death!" A very 'active' prayer.

But I am thinking more of the simplicity and attitude of prayer in our daily lives. Once we have this, then the events of each day, however outwardly difficult, assume almost a secondary place in the overall sense of peace in God's will - "In His will is our peace" as Dante wrote. And this is not a shallow sort of complacency, but comes from the acceptance and certainty that God is at the heart of the world.

How do we acquire this certainty? How, too, in the climate of today's unruly and often decadent world, can we assume that God is at the heart of it? The short answer, I suppose, is *faith*. Always, in both the Old and New Testaments, it was faith that was rewarded. Think of Abraham and Isaac. Abraham's faith was put to the ultimate test when he prepared to sacrifice his son (a foreshadowing of the Crucifixion) and look at the outcome: 'I will shower blessings on you,' God told Abraham, 'and your descendants will be as many as the stars of heaven and the grains of sand on the sea shore.' The whole history of the Jews stemmed from those great fathers, Moses, Abraham and Isaac, in the Old Testament. In the New Testament, of course, faith is constantly marked: Mary's faith - 'be it done to me according to thy word' - and by Jesus on countless occasions: 'Go in peace, thy faith hath made thee whole. - '

So how do we *find* the faith that brings the certainty of God's presence, and is thereby the root of our prayer? We have some very authentic guides. We have the *Church*. We have the promise of *Jesus*: 'Know that I am with you always, yes, to the end of time,' and we have the *Scriptures*, with their cycle of battles won and lost, their stories of failures, stupidities, incomprehensions - all reminiscent again and again of today's ill-adjusted world, ill-adjusted because God gave us free will and never *forced* us to love him. And through it all is the enduring encouragement of Jesus' words before the Last Supper: 'I am the Way, the Truth and the Life...I tell you most solemnly, whoever believes in me will perform the same works as I do myself, because I am going to the Father... Anyone who loves me will be loved by my Father, and I shall love him and show myself to him.' (St John 14)

And today he shows himself to us not as he did to St Thomas: 'Put your finger here; look, here are my hands. Doubt no longer but believe.' He says it in the gift of himself in Communion, in the sacraments. He gives us *Himself*. And as if that were not enough, we were given the Holy Spirit to be our constant companion. 'Come Holy Spirit, fill the hearts of your faithful, and enkindle within them the fire of your *love*', we pray at Pentecost.

All these immeasurable gifts are ours - and we neglect them at our cost. Once we have begun to catch even a glimpse of the immensity of God's love for us, we have activated, so to speak, the *sense* of his presence. Thus we are motivated to pray so that the jagged pieces of our lives, and those of the world, will fall into the mosaic that we shall one day perceive in its entirety.

And where does *pain* come into all this? Pain that is not brought about by selfishness, but seems an unsought adjunct of our humanity? What about the young mother afflicted by cancer, the untimely death of a child, the slow deterioration of mind for those who succumb to Alzheimer's disease, or any of the decimating illnesses prevalent today? There are so many inexplicable agonies for which there are no rational explanations. We are back again to faith. We do not understand. Despite our prayer, the loved friend does not recover, a husband dies, the baby is born with cerebral palsy.

And *still* we have to cling to faith. We cannot pretend about pain. Pain *hurts*. It is there, raw, unassuageable. We can rail against God: 'If that's the way you treat your friends, no wonder you have so few!' as St Teresa of Avila remonstrated, and we can weep at the seeming discrepancy between pain and the God of Love we are taught to revere. Yet - we are followers of Christ, and it is Christ who shows us the way of the Cross. It is through the Cross on our own particular road that we are brought to the full measure of our humanity.

And here is the paradox: it is in the acceptance, *in faith*, of our pain - our Cross - that we become aware of the risen Christ beside us. He is there, he has gone before us, he *knows* us, and nothing - *nothing* - need separate us from his love. We begin to see his hand in everything, even adversity, which He allows to overtake us - but only so that we shall find it in Him.

THOUGHT FOR THE DAY –
BBC Radio Sussex

A greater spotted woodpecker came to the nut-holder hanging in my garden on Christmas morning. I looked out of the window and there he was, an unexpected, lovely Christmas present. I'd never seen one here before, and his beauty enchanted me - that great splash of scarlet and his black and white plumage when he turned his back, almost swinging upside down in his determination to reach the nuts. The customary blue tits appeared really rattled waiting for him to finish. And he didn't hurry. It was quite ten minutes before he flew off in great swift bounds.

The strange thing about that woodpecker was his appearance on Christmas morning. You see, the elderly friend I used to visit in North Devon also loved birds, and one of her particular joys was in providing for the numerous variety visiting her garden from nearby woods. Among these was a greater spotted woodpecker, and although I never actually saw him myself when staying with her, she would often ring me up to tell me he had been there that day. She felt very honoured that he should visit her.

This elderly friend had a second stroke in November, and early in December she died, and I missed her. There was no customary card from her this year, no telephone call. But on Christmas morning when I saw from my window that greater spotted woodpecker, how could I doubt who had organised his coming? It was Nell's Christmas present!

THOUGHT FOR THE DAY –
BBC Radio Sussex

Mark is my next door neighbour's cross/cairn terrier. As a pup of eight weeks he was given to a family wanting a dog, and we missed him.

A year later they brought young Mark back, now grown and rough-haired. "We're afraid he's no good -" they said. "We can't keep him. He's bad-tempered and growls and we're afraid he might even snap -"

It was hard to believe anything so small could be unlovable. Then they explained. Apparently, though much admired, he was a pet for everyone - and no one's in particular. When he growled, they had even called a dog psychologist who recommended shaking him by the scruff of his neck each time he did so, with the result that no one could approach him. They left him with my neighbour.

When I saw him again after his return, I bent down to welcome him. "Urrrr" he scowled, so I left him and walked away. The next morning, as I was washing-up, he appeared round the open kitchen door. "Feeling better?" I enquired. He accepted half a biscuit and all but grinned.

Now, eighteen months later, feeling secure, he has become a sunny little dog, loved and cared for by his owner, though a bit possessive. Don't try taking away his toys. But the transformation is huge.

I suppose that's the thing about love. The classic case of response to security and so on. Seeing the potential is often almost impossible because of all sorts of off-putting external circumstances. And it is easy to make snap judgements!

I remember the poem by Francis Thompson. "'Tis ye, 'tis your estranged faces, That miss the many splendored thing."

Things *are* many-splendored. Not only obvious ones like butterflies and the dew on spiders' webs in September, but in the unsuspected crevices of life too. Look at the rainbow colours in the bubbles of your washing-up liquid. (It doesn't matter which brand!)

THOUGHT FOR THE DAY –
BBC Radio Sussex

I have to wait till March to prune the roses in my garden. We are so exposed to the strong wind that it is touch and go to get the new leaf-buds through without their being shrivelled by the blast.

The other morning was so still and shiny that I took a chance and went round snipping. (I'd learned how to find the outward facing bud, and all the proper 'cuts', from the garden sister in the community). Bar impaling my thumb on a large thorn and scratching my chin as I bent to inspect a stem, I got the whole lot done before so much as a breeze threatened the operation.

Haven't you found that events in life so often have a 'pruning' effect? Dreadfully unwelcome at the time, we cringe when anything appears to be 'lopped off'. Letting go is never pleasant - possessions, children, even chocolate during Lent - yet how often, time after time, we come across people who have borne real adversity. Far from diminishment, their capacity for understanding or compassion seems to have been hugely enlarged.

I think of a Romanian friend who experienced great deprivation at the time of their revolution. She works tirelessly now for Romanian orphans. Another, whose son died tragically, is always the first to welcome the lonely or unhappy. There are so many instances. We all know of them.

When I marvel anew at the beauty of those roses in June, I'm reminded of that human paradox. Pruning does make a difference.

From a Quiet Day at Hunston

One of you suggested that we could share this day with the accent on faith. Might I, for what they are worth, give you a few thoughts of my own on this great subject? Afterwards perhaps we can have some questions or discussion, depending on when I run out of steam!

I was in Lourdes last year, helping with sick pilgrims and finding myself often in the ward of one of the hospices. A middle-aged woman came in one afternoon, she told me she was from Manchester. She was not a Catholic, but had come to help with night duty. She told me she was a trained nurse. We started talking, and she asked if we might meet later that evening before she went on duty. We found our way to a café in due course, and she said "You know, I just can't think what it is about this place. It's full of contradictions. Those dreadfully trashy souvenir stalls, crowds all pushing like a day at the Sales, the discomfort of it all - and yet there's this amazing faith. My mother," she went on, "would turn in her grave to think of me here -"

I found myself running through a sort of history of the Church, pointing out the similarities between Lourdes, with all its contradictions, and the choice of St Peter, appointed by Christ despite his human frailties. Both Lourdes and St Peter were, I said, infused with grace contrary to outward appearance. I then had the temerity to suggest that it might even be her mother, now with the clear vision of eternity, who had possibly had a hand in her coming to Lourdes! "You still think of your mother as she *was*", I began - and before I could say any more she exclaimed "And I should be seeing her as she *is*!"

Faith, I believe, is the seeing of things as they are, despite outward appearance. Look at the snap judgements we make!

We size up someone, act on that decision, never knowing what might have taken place within that soul: fears, sadnesses, inherited traits and tendencies. Their faith may have been enormous under *their* circumstances, our own abysmally inadequate.

The faith that so struck my friend in Lourdes was, of course, evident. Sick pilgrims struggling to reach the Grotto, their faith indeed rewarded - spiritually certainly, and sometimes physically. 'Go in peace,' said Christ, 'thy faith hath made thee whole...'

But what is this faith? How do we know we have it - and, if we feel we haven't, how do we get it?

'Faith', said. St Paul, 'is the substance of things hoped for.' (A modern translation has 'the guarantee of the blessings we hope for' Hebrews 11). You remember how Abraham, called to sacrifice his son (or so he supposed) actually laid Isaac upon the stone and raised the knife before the angel intervened. Abraham's faith was tested to the limit (let alone Isaac's!) and then, only after that, was he deemed fit to obey the call to set out for the promised land - not even knowing where he was going.

But what about ourselves? Well of course we do have faith - for without faith we should never cross a room, nor live through the day - but isn't the sort of faith we feel we should like for ourselves more a sense - a comfortable awareness - a 'money in the bank' sort of certainty, a promise of sunshine for the holiday weekend, a faith that of *course* there is life after death, like a ticket in advance?

That is *our* way. God's way for us may be quite different! We are speaking of faith that helps to make us grow, the faith we were promised at our baptism. It is not forced on us against our will, but is for us to pray for, a gift given, and we can equally disregard it or let it drift away. So to grow in faith, I think we have to grow in prayer - to grow in that union with God for which we were created. We begin by recognising our *need* to pray, so that eventually prayer becomes a continual 'raising of our hearts and mind to God' in every situation. Not only those 'holy' moments, but in the scattered moments of the day when everything around us feels like a distraction.

It is all a question, I think, of how we *look*. God *is* everywhere, whether you are aware of it or not, but if we can train ourselves to notice him in his 'indwelling' of creation, our minds will eventually be concentrated on the reality of his presence at all times. And that in turn creates faith. You can say, in your heart, '*I know*'.

All those people you hear about who have remarkable 'answers to prayer', or take on the building of houses or the purchase of this or that necessity and come up a week later with the exact amount needed 'out of the blue', have, let's face it, faith. But they have also, I suspect, encouraged the growth of that faith, by pretty constant prayer. So, you see, prayer is the key. (We know this, really.) Praying unlocks the door and faith enters. Then, at last, we have the assurance we craved. And we come to see that we are not alone in our struggle. Our lives are lived under the shadow of God's providential love, however bumpy or full of potholes that path may seem to other eyes. We are each given the strength we need for our own particular road. And God is there, within us and in others around us. We can trust implicitly in his promise, which is no less than 'eternal life for all those that love him and keep his commandments...'

THOUGHT FOR THE DAY –
BBC Radio Sussex

Coming down from Scotland on the Inter-City train most of the seats were reserved - or so it seemed to me from the forest of little cards waving from every row in the carriage. I was glad I'd taken advice and booked my own.

The seat beside me was still unoccupied even after we'd passed the station from which it was reserved, so I pointed this out to a woman I saw making her way down the aisle in a vain attempt to find a place, and she slipped in beside me, thankfully.

We did not speak much until she offered me her newspaper and then - as so often when travelling - we began to talk of current events which led, eventually, to more personal anecdotes. She told me of her family, the garden, the animals she kept, and I explained some of my own work as a religious and so on. A cousin of hers was ill and she asked me to pray for him - we even discovered we had friends in common, which amazed us. It was a small world. Before we knew where we were, we had reached King's Cross and our ways parted.

That's what I like about life. How easy it is to go about the whole thing, one's nose to the ground, concentrating on one's own narrow path - yet making room for someone, whether actually or simply by an attitude, is so much more rewarding!

There was a 'party piece' by Eleanor Farjeon I was often called upon to recite in the community. It was a poem: '*Mrs Malone*' and continued for quite a few verses, each verse ending "'There's room for another' said Mrs Malone" - and I suddenly remembered it when I moved over on that crowded train the other week.

I think there always *is* room for another, when you come to think of it.

THOUGHT FOR THE DAY –
BBC Radio Sussex

I looked through a box of old photographs recently. You know the kind I mean - rather faded black and white, curled at the edges and showing set-looking objects and groups of relatives in comic poses, all long since gone. I felt a sense of nostalgia for those remembered times: long summer hours by the sea, quiet days in the garden. Nothing seemed hurried.

Near the bottom of the box I came across a scrap of paper and recognised my grandmother's writing. "Gone to the hayfield", she'd written, and I wondered for whom the note was intended, and why it had found its way into the photograph box and not been consigned to the dustbin.

I have a much more recent photograph of sisters in my community raking hay in the old orchard. With habits pinned up and old straw hats flopping over their nuns' veiling, they appear even further from the past than any of' those in my box.

Isn't it marvellous to think that year after year, season after season, Spring comes again - just as it always has. Remembered fields might now be submerged by motorway or housing estate, mechanical rakes make light work of remaining silage or sundried hay - but still that moment comes when the first pink blossom shows. Suddenly there are new leaves breaking at the tips of the lime tree, a blackbird singing his heart out on a branch of the lilac.

It reminds me of a poem by V.L. Edmondson, written almost as long ago as my old photographs were printed:

'God, you have made a very perfect world,
Don't let me spoil it ever any more.'

THOUGHT FOR THE DAY –
BBC Radio Sussex

A friend has just returned from her son's wedding to a Japanese girl. The wedding took place in Tokyo and she had made every effort to get there for her son's special day.

I saw her the other morning and she was full of the totally new experience. Although small herself, she found herself looking down on most of her son's in-laws, which gave her quite a boost. Telling me of the details of her stay, she couldn't get over the kindness and consideration shown her, particularly making me laugh by describing her visit, with her hostess, to the public bath.

This bath, she told me, was frequently taken and you went together, stripping off in a cubicle before proceeding, towel over arm, to the actual washing place. There, she explained, you tipped little bowls of water over yourself, soaping all over, chatting to your friend or neighbour, before progressing to a really hot filled bath, a sort of jacuzzi, in which you immersed yourself up to the chin. Later you repaired to the dressing room to continue chatting over tea - or whatever appropriate refreshment was to hand.

I was delighted to learn of the different culture and customs, and thrilled with the brightly coloured fan she brought me as a memento.

A few months ago this friend's husband had died very suddenly. I was at the funeral. It had been very moving, and everyone had been as supportive as they could - yet no one can take away that pain of loss, not the grief after all those years of marriage. She had made an immense effort to accompany her son to Japan so soon afterwards, thinking only of his happiness.

Here she was, home again, and revitalised by her experience. She *might* have shut herself in, nursing her grief, and everyone would have felt sad for her. That wasn't her way. She *opened* the door and went out to meet life - and came back full of love and that precious gift, laughter.

From an address to the Union of Catholic Mothers

Unless a grain of wheat falls into the ground and dies, it remains only a single grain; but if it dies, it yields a rich harvest. (John 12 v 24)

We are the husk. During our lives, the growth of what seems our importance, our social position - this is the outer part of ourselves, the part that gives us our confidence in the world. Only when we become old or dependent on others does that outer covering perhaps gradually become discarded. Only then do we begin to catch a glimpse of the inner shell - the kernel.

I often find myself visiting the elderly in a variety of homes, and it is striking to notice the differing attitudes. One ninety year old who was always ready to smile, told me how much she appreciated this time of waiting in what she called 'the ante-room'. "It gives me time to think -" she said, "and I love to rest in that hope I sense so clearly -" (I forgot to mention that she is very nearly blind.) I always take the most scented bunch from the garden so that she can guess each sprig or flower from its smell.

Another, quite a bit younger, is totally different. Whenever I visit she immediately grumbles, usually about the quality of the staff, and always refuses flowers because they "take up too much space". She hates her life, and complains that "God hasn't taken me yet -"

Of course this is all to do with temperament - but I think it can also be an indication of what the 'inner life', the kernel, has become. We are created for our union with God, and if our entire life is spent concentrating only on outwardly important things (to us) then we are running on empty when that outer husk begins to shrivel. Oh, of *course* there is God's infinite mercy at the end, but how much happier (for everyone) it is when the inner spiritual growth reveals itself.

After Palm Sunday and that procession of Jesus to Jerusalem with all its acclaim, the disciples expected the Messianic kingdom to come quickly. Here was their Master - and they were on the winning side! They did not understand at all. Suddenly the whole thing appeared to collapse and they were left with a King who did not even defend himself, whose 'kingdom' seemed to dissolve before their eyes. Peter even denied him three times.

They had only taken in his *outward* appearance, the husk of his humanity.

It was not until after his death and crucifixion, when he was nailed to the cross, that his redemptive act was revealed. Slow to understand, at last they caught a glimpse of the reality. Jesus *was* indeed God's son. He had come to assume the sins of the world in his humanity, in order to redeem them. His 'kernel' had been divine all along.

We can so understand those disciples! What an anti-climax. Only so slowly did the penny drop as little by little they came to grasp something of the vastness of his kingdom. Thomas, in the twentieth chapter of St John's gospel, told them "Unless I see the mark of the nails in his hands...I will not believe."

Let us remember Thomas. We can easily relate to his incredulity. Let us ask that our own lives, inwardly and outwardly, be strengthened so that our husk (and the kernel) are receptive to the power of God's pervading love.

THOUGHT FOR THE DAY –
BBC Radio Sussex

I went to visit a new-born baby the other day. He was asleep in his mother's arms, a tiny bundle with long eyelashes and downy hair and those wonderfully small hands, curled and content, oblivious to all around him. It was almost impossible to imagine him eventually six feet tall and flying to Australia or riding a motorbike or any of the probable occupations he might one day pursue. Now he relied entirely on his parents. They were his means of survival. His trust in them was total.

And it was only yesterday that I had a letter from a friend in America. She is ninety-two and I have never met her, but we have corresponded ever since she wrote to the community and I was given the letter to answer.

Now she wrote to thank me for the airletter I'd sent last month. It was only towards its close that she told me of her daughter's illness and went on, "Alas, I cannot get to her, my travelling days are over. I could not make the journey now." I know from her letters that this elderly friend has enormous faith. She relies on this, and reaches out in it to all whom she knows and loves. In that faith she accepts the events that touch her daily life and her serenity is evident, more and more so as the years pass.

I couldn't help comparing that week-old baby with the ninety-two year old American, one at the beginning of life, the other coming towards its close. Both were reliant on others for daily necessities.

I should like that baby to reach as serene an old age as my unseen elderly friend, with faith as shining as hers.

THOUGHT FOR THE DAY –
BBC Radio Sussex

They have been bringing in the harvest recently. The combine harvester crawls up the lane near where I live and field by field the grain is gathered, leaving only those huge straw- bales in its wake.

David, the farmer, told me the grain wasn't too good this year - too much damping - but he was glad to have a fine stretch to get the harvest in, and there was a large crop.

As I walked up the hill I thought of the loaf I'd bought from the supermarket. In its neatly printed cellophane pack, sliced thin, medium or thick, brown, white or 'harvest fresh with grain included' it all seemed remote from those fields.

When 'travellers' called at my convent, we always offered bread, cheese and a mug of tea. Bread is a symbol of life, bread sustains, bread is a sign of communion. We used to make our own, and the smell of newly-baked bread was something I'll always remember.

Then I think of famine in the world - at the moment it is in Ethiopia - and of those photographs of shrivelled dried-up shoots of corn in places where no rain comes. I cringe when I remember the times I throw out bread that has become stale, and of those uneaten bits left on plates after a meal. Where there is plenty, waste seems of such small importance.

Coming home past those fields in the evening light, the long shadows, the stubble still gold, it struck me how unthinking we could be about our daily lives. Not only in the wasting of bread or food, but of all the other things we take for granted - friends and relationships and love - and even of life itself.

We each have a harvest to gather.

From a talk to the CWL at Arundel

Today being the lovely feast of the Assumption, two particular thoughts came to my mind: the first was the passage by St Bernard where he writes of the Annunciation:

The angel is waiting for your answer.
We too are waiting, O Lady...answer, O
Virgin, answer the angel speedily;
rather, through the angel, answer
your Lord. Speak the word and receive
the Word...offer what is yours and
conceive what is of God; give what is
temporal and embrace what is eternal.

Those lines led me to the thought of the indwelling of the Holy Spirit. (Have you ever considered how different the outcome might have been had Mary *not* said 'be it done according to thy word'...?) And how the Holy Spirit really does dwell in us. And, if he dwells in us, he is there with all his gifts - nothing half-hearted about the Holy Spirit!

How often, it seems to me, we forget all about this indwelling. We could make so much more use of him! We bumble along so busily, engulfed in our preoccupations and quite forget to 'press the button' that activates the grace within us. For I believe we *do* have to activate it, consciously centering ourselves, so to speak, so that we bring to mind the grace and strength and courage we need.

The other day, knowing I wanted time to get down some notes for a quiet day I was due to conduct, I found myself engulfed with all sorts of unforeseen things: people turned up to stay or rang in trouble or wanted to be met off the train just when I should have been somewhere else, and I became resentful inside because I could get no time to think. In my external fuss, I burned the milk saucepan and snapped at poor Cherry, the next door collie, and even cut my thumb with the potato peeler. I was altogether steamed up. I even said my prayers hustling: 'don't let it be said I left out my prayers, Lord!' I remonstrated. Then at last I gave up and stopped trying to do two things at once and tried to concentrate on the matter in hand. Of course *this* was what the Holy Spirit had wanted - not my fussing about a talk I was giving next week. (He has given me space now, you see!)

Somewhere along the line I'm sure we have to learn to become aware of that presence within... I am for ever quoting that verse from the psalms: 'Be still and know that I am God...' and I am sure this is the answer. This 'being still' wherein we actually silence ourselves and try to listen. Quite difficult. We sit quietly and the shopping list or tomorrow's lunch keeps cropping up. But I think the very fact of our wanting to give that moment - or more than a moment - is in itself an act of will which triggers the grace we are talking about. And the remarkable fact is that whatever we subsequently find ourselves doing, will be done *under the Holy Spirit's guidence*. And the reward and joy of that consequence is that everything about our meagre effort becomes transformed - base metal to gold - by Him. In fact St Paul had it about right when he wrote 'I of myself can do nothing - but I can do all things through Christ which strengtheneth me...'

THOUGHT FOR THE DAY –
BBC Radio Sussex

For the last few mornings, I've come downstairs to find the tell-tale tracks of a snail across the sitting-room carpet. I live in the depths of the country, and much as I like most living creatures, I have to confess that snails are not one of my favourites. Not in the garden, and emphatically not in the sitting-room.

Unable to find the actual intruder, I sprinkled salt round the carpet edge and under the garden door (someone once said it was a cure) and brushed away the offending trail. Next morning there it was again. It was shining in the morning sun.

"Where *are* you?" I lamented, on my hands and knees. Could he merely come for the night, weave about drunkenly and take himself off at daybreak to sleep it off?

As I clutched my dressing-gown tightly, it occurred to me how persevering was that small creature, its house on its back, its strange attraction to my sitting-room unwavering despite my declared warfare with the salt. I couldn't bring myself to any sort of liking for it, but somewhere I did begin to sense a sort relationship with my unseen invader. He had something.

I know a lot of people - myself included - who get dreadfully despondent over quite small slights in life. The remarks made by someone and interpreted as insulting, or the feeling of sheer offence when one is beaten to a parking space. At the first sign of deterrent, let alone salt, I should have given up, rebelled, blamed someone else.

Tracking down my snail – *trying* to track down my snail - I found myself smiling. "OK -" I said. "You've won this time.

But watch it! You have *taught* me something -" And I recalled that old eastern proverb I'd come across years ago:

By patience and perseverance, and a bottle of sweet oil, the snail at last reaches Jerusalem.

But I still wish it need not be via my sitting-room.

Quiet Day for the Oasis Group
at Duncton Manor

"The fear of the Lord is the beginning of wisdom" from psalm 111 verse 10 (and much the same wording from Proverbs, chapter 1.)

In his introduction to the 'Wisdom' books in the Jerusalem Bible - Job, Proverbs, Ecclesiastes and Wisdom - the editing scholar tells us that these books continued a tradition that stretched back throughout the ancient East. 'Wisdom' treated of the meaning of life, it offered a recipe for successful living. The sages of Israel, however, viewed this 'Wisdom' in the light of Yahweh, of God. Though the 'Wisdom' of Israel resembles the common 'Wisdom' of the East, it has an essential superiority, and the contrast between wisdom and folly becomes an opposition between virtue and vice, between true religion and false. Real 'Wisdom' is found in the fear of God 'which is the very foundation of true religion. The 'Wisdom' of the East may be called humanistic. The 'Wisdom' of Israel is humanism spiritualised.

But I would like to return to those texts in a moment.

A few weeks ago I had the great good fortune of spending five days in Florence, and of the many wonderful churches and museums I most wanted to visit was San Marco, with its frescoes by Fra Angelico.

Of course everyone is familiar with the reproductions of Fra Angelico's work on Christmas and Easter cards, but I hadn't recalled seeing 'The Transfiguration' before, and I was particularly struck by the detail - which I would love you to see - of Saint Peter. As it says in the accompanying text: "The fresco fully expresses the sense of the disturbing vision experienced by Peter, James and John on Mount Tabor in Galilee."

One sees in Peter's expression that mixture of perplexity and awe, that all too human reaction to a vision so far removed from everyday experience. Did that insight, however incomprehensible, give Peter an assurance? When the time of Jesus' crucifixion came, did he remember again what he had been permitted to witness? He might have supposed he had been mistaken: there appeared no 'glory' in the Crucifixion. Even when asked by Jesus, "Lovest thou me?" he had no conception of the task that lay before him. And we know the rest: Peter the Rock. The Church. *Saint* Peter, and the long unfolding of Christianity, right through to ourselves.

Then we have St Paul. He also had to be knocked for six - so much so that he was literally felled to the ground en route to Damascus. Another 'sight of the glory'. In St Paul's case, it led to his endless journeys of evangelisation, his letters and his thundering to all with whom he came in contact "God's plan is to make known his secret to his people, and the secret is that *Christ is in you.*" Christ - the Light of the world - the *light*.

I believe we all need this glimpse of the 'glory', the 'light', before we can go forward in our lives with something like certainty. It gives us a confidence that there is something greater than ourselves - the 'Christ in you' to strengthen and enable. To be personal for a moment, I shall never forget the day I actually committed myself to enter the convent. I had been unsure and wobbly, but as I walked down the hill having fixed the date to make that leap in my life, I was overwhelmed with a sense of intense joy and a wonderful perception of light. Of course it only lasted a day or two, and very soon I was propelled into the emotional upheaval and preparation for life in an enclosed convent, but that sense of 'light' and an acceptance of one's calling upheld me through many times of difficulty.

And that is another thing. There will *always* be times of difficulty. We were never promised an easy path. Some of us, some more than others, are asked to endure great burdens. Yet we are given courage, and we glimpse through the glass however darkly sometimes, and see that we are not alone. Have you noticed how frequently when we are at rock-bottom there will be a hand held out perhaps, or a smile, or even a tame blackbird (like the one that comes into my room when I am on the telephone!)

Let us return to that 'fear of the Lord' we mentioned. It is easily misinterpreted in modern language. Fear is equated with fright, and unpleasantness, and the sense of an 'icy hand' at the throat. But, as we realise in the biblical context, fear is associated with awe and the immensity of God's manifestations to Moses and Abraham and those great Jewish fathers. They realised they were in the presence of God and fell on their faces before him. 'Fear of the Lord' -

In her Revelations of Divine Love, the fourteenth century mystic Dame Julian of Norwich has chapter after chapter on Our Lord's love. We are led by her 'visions' to an understanding of the *endless* love he has for us. "Truth", she writes, "seeth God, and Wisdom beholdeth God, and of these two cometh the third: that is, a holy marvellous delight in God, which is Love. Where Truth and Wisdom are verily, there is Love verily, coming of them both. And all of God's making, for he is endless sovereign Truth, endless sovereign Wisdom, endless sovereign Love, un-made; (uncreated) and man's Soul is a creature in God which hath the same properties *made* (created) and evermore it doth what it was made for: it seeth God, it beholdeth God, and it loveth God. Wherefore God enjoyeth in the creature; and the creature in God, endlessly marvelling."

So here we are, back to the 'fear of God is the beginning of Wisdom'. In fact it is all one thing. The whole purpose of life is to gain an understanding of that Love. Our failures usually come when we forget this - so easy in this materialistic world. I was taken to the Wintershall 'Life of Christ' the other day. I joined the three thousand watching that amazing depiction (in the rain as it happened!) and found myself speculating on those hundreds of schoolchildren. How much, I wondered, are they going to retain of that 'Life' in their own lives? Perhaps, I found myself praying, they will have experienced a spark of that Gospel teaching. A faint echo, maybe, of the disturbing vision we witnessed in the expression of Peter in Fra Angelico's fresco.

Quiet Day for the Oasis Group at Duncton Manor

I heard part of a radio service the other day in which the preacher mentioned the word 'readiness'. This started off a train of thought which, I suppose, applies to us all: and I remembered John the Baptist and his "Prepare the way of the Lord..."

That collect from the first Sunday of Advent begins "Stir up our hearts, O Lord, to prepare the ways of your only-begotten Son -"

In ancient times, in the East, when a great potentate was going on a journey, the way was, quite literally, levelled before him, a straight way cut, obstacles cleared. (Sounds awfully like one's garden.) When, after many weeks, the road was ready for the immediate journey, a forerunner was sent ahead to shout warning and clear the path of chickens, goats and small children.

Today, as Christians, of course we consider ourselves prepared, through the teachings of the New Testament, to the extent that we accept and believe. But we still need *faith*.

Of course, without one aspect of that word, faith, we should never put a foot out of bed, nor undertake the hundred and one events each day brings. One has *faith* that the kettle will boil or the bath water run from the tap. That is the simple application of the word.

But the faith I am thinking about is the God-given *gift* of faith, and for that we can apply the 'readiness'. We must be *ready* to receive the gift of faith.

The origin of Christian faith was the biblical faith of Abraham. He had pledged his existence by his faith in God's promise of innumerable descendants. He had left his own land and become converted. We can read the account of this in Genesis (Chapter 12).

We also have the lovely story of Sarah being told she would conceive long after she could have done so naturally. And from her springs Isaac - and the unfolding and ups and downs of the whole Old Testament story of faith.

St Paul, in his letter to Timothy, indicates that the priceless gift of faith can be frittered away, or lost. "Hold faith and a good conscience," he writes. "By rejecting conscience, certain persons have made a shipwreck of their faith... " (I got that translation from the New Catechism.)

Conscience is a tricky one! Have I put faith at risk by telling a whopper or 'forgetting' to return that book I borrowed (filched) from its owner? One hopes not enough to cause shipwreck, but one gets the point.

St James has a pretty strong opinion about faith. In his Letter (chapter 2) he writes "What doth it profit, my brethren, though a man says he hath faith and hath not works? Can faith save him?" I looked this up in the Message Bible that Susie gave me last year (page 484). "Dear Friends, do you think you'll get anywhere in this if you learn all the right words but never do anything? Does merely talking about faith indicate that a person really has it?"

We get the gist!

Even though enlightened by him in whom one believes, faith is often lived in darkness - and can be put to the test (like Abraham and Isaac again, for instance, and many of those other great patriarchs of the Old Testament.) What we see and hear around us in today's unattractive conditions can easily shake our faith, especially if the foundations are at all wobbly. Faith *has* to be tested, often again and again.

Then we have the 'faith' required for the miracles worked by Jesus. "Behold thy *faith* hath healed thee -" In these cases the faith came from a belief that was probably based on hearsay (rather as we are recommended a doctor or an acupuncturist or any sort of healer). Only later did it dawn - in some cases - that this was a very different sort of healer. The faith of the disciples was rather like this: a slow comprehension and gradual unfolding of love for Christ. And even this was severely put to the test at the crucifixion, just when they were counting on temporal victory, a sort of World Cup.

I remember so clearly when I first had my leave of absence from the convent, the huge leap in the dark it felt. Not *quite* Abraham leaving his own land, but definitely a sense of taking one's toe off the bottom of the pool when learning to swim. You may remember my describing the death from cancer of the friend I had thought to be working with, and then the death of her husband, all within three months. Quite a 'deep end' experience. I could never have coped were it not for the long habit of prayer and faith imbibed from my community. I recall saying in a sanctimonious way "Faith isn't faith unless it is taking steps in the dark..." True. And I know that for you, too, there have been times of great pain to endure, whether physical or spiritual, and I think you will have come to know the truth of these 'steps in the dark'. I am sure that we can seldom see the way ahead, or make some sort of military plan. One either says "You show me, Lord," and trusts, or goes along without recourse to him. Did I ever share with you that prayer to the Holy Spirit? I say it daily, and it has made a tangible difference to my life:

O Holy Spirit, soul of my soul, I adore you.
Enlighten, guide, strengthen and console me,
Tell me what I ought to do and command me to do it.
I promise to submit to everything you ask of me
and to accept all you allow to happen to me.
Just show me what is your will.

So I think we can equate that 'readiness' I mentioned with the importance of nurturing our faith, for faith is born from the readiness to accept. And as I am sure each of us here today is only too aware of this, I think we all long to be ensured of that *infinite* love God longs for us to perceive. It is his gift for us. And all down the centuries we see the examples of this love, this faith, in God.

This readiness. Look at the early martyrs. Nothing, not even fire or sword or rack, could separate them from their love of him.

With a bit of luck, we shall not be asked to endure too much of that - though this sort of martyrdom is never too far away today. But we *can* work, or try to work, consciously at increasing our readiness and faith, and our *certainty* in the unending care God has for each of us. There is a prayer I found, it is from a Methodist manual I think, and I wrote it down to share with you.

> We are no longer our own but yours.
> Put us to what you will, rank us with whom you will;
> put us to doing, put us to suffering;
> let us be employed for you, or laid aside for you,
> exalted for you, or brought low for you;
> let us be full, let us be empty;
> let us have all things, let us have nothing.
> We freely and wholeheartedly yield all things
> to your pleasure and disposal.
>
> And now, glorious and blessed God,
> Father, Son and Holy Spirit,
> you are ours and we are yours
> So be it.
> And the covenant which we made on earth,
> let it be ratified in heaven.

Which brings me, as always, to my dear Julian of Norwich, to whom I fly at all times, like a homing pigeon:

'And thus I understood that what man or woman with firm will chooseth God in this life, for love, he may be sure that he is loved without end: which endless love worketh in him that grace. For he willeth that we be as assured in hope of the bliss of heaven while we are here, as we shall in sureness while we are there.'

That's worth preparing for, making a bit of readiness for, don't you agree?

Quiet Day for the Oasis Group
at Duncton Manor

When Tuëma told me that you had suggested I shared with you a few thoughts on dying, and the coming through to eternal life, I almost smiled. How typical, I thought, of the Holy Spirit to come up with the one topic for which, over the recent weeks, I had become all too familiar - and not for the first time.

Towards the end of Lent this year, I had been invited to lead a small retreat for a mixed house group. I had begun by suggesting that it was not the denial of ginger biscuits so much as the acceptance of what befalls us, which is the safer way of uniting ourselves with him whom one loves. (No smugness, as one might get with the denial of ginger biscuits.) The operative word in this matter of 'accepting', I suggested, was the *love* to which one was striving to unite oneself.

Recently I had been telephoned by the 'partner' of a female couple in the town, asking if I could visit her dying friend who was in some fear and understandable distress. I had seen them in the town but could hardly have said I knew them, and it was with some apprehension, that I was led upstairs to where the friend, terribly emaciated - she had pancreatic cancer - lay propped up in bed. She managed a weak smile and put out a hand to me. She told me she *thought* she believed in God, but that was about all. She also knew she was dying.

"I want, if I can, to help you not to be frightened," I said. "Not easy, but perhaps it might help a little if we can share this 'waiting-room' time". I did not stay long: I was afraid of tiring her. I promised to come whenever she wished me to visit.

In the event, I was there every day for five weeks, watching her illness take its toll, reassuring her to the best of my ability.

It was inspiring to become acquainted with the amazingly dedicated MacMillan nurses, as well as the district nurses, who called regularly. Towards the end, a special bed was placed in the sitting-room and eventually she slipped away, with my promise that 'all shall be well' a comfort, I hope, as she made that transition into a life more permanent than this one. She died on Pentecost Sunday.

Of course accepting the dark pain of bereavement is an agony in every way. Anyone who has experienced this will know only too well. For Lucy, the partner who was left, all I could say was that perhaps she, being better able to manage, was being asked to remain. It was a crumb of comfort, but at least the shadow of a reason, though there is never a cast-iron reply to the ways of God. Only very much later, with hindsight, can any sort of pattern be observed.

Years of study and learning in the convent had steeped me in the certainty of God's indwelling love. I *knew* the translation of the soul from its mortal body was no more a permanent 'death' than a butterfly emerging from its chrysalis. The nearest analogy, I suppose, is of birth: the warm comfort of the womb has signified total security to the unborn baby. I think what most assails us is the fear of the unknown. We have no 'experience' of what awaits us. We are afraid of leaving the familiar environment. But have you not noticed, it is almost always when viewed from afar that death has this icy grip on our imagination? Just as for the baby, I think, when the time comes this 'birth' is a natural consequence in fact. I have seen this very often.

Once we catch a glimpse of the meaning of God's indwelling love - his love *within* us - the eternal life of the soul that is absolutely unquenchable because it is forever in the mind of God - then we can more easily grasp that nothing, ever, can be lost. I suspect even those who have done unutterable evil in their lives are not lost to God. There will be a great deal to work at before they are aware, or can even bear, the eternal light of his love - but there is no time in what we call heaven. *Nothing* need separate us from the love of God. It is only we ourselves who are sometimes carelessly blind to it.

As you may recall, I often quote from Julian of Norwich, whose writings in the fifteenth century so reverberate with the love of God, and God's love for us. "See", she quotes from one of her 'revelations', "See, I never lift my hands off my works, nor ever shall, world without end. See, I lead all things to the end I ordain it to, from without-beginning, with the same might, wisdom and love that I made it with. How should anything be amiss?"

When we see so much suffering in the world, the horrors of war, the victims of famine, the lonely, those ravaged by drugs, we wonder in agony why these evils are not prevented by God. But - thought through - is it not we ourselves, the human race, who bear responsibility here? Were we not given free will, and time after time, over thousands of years, have we not forgotten how 'sweetly and tenderly' our Maker loves us? Beguiled by material benefits, by the mirage of success, by our own sin and selfishness, I think we have all added to the snowball of sin in the world. We were not 'prevented' because God had given us this free will, and allowed us to take responsibility for our actions. As the poet Francis Thompson wrote: "'tis ye, 'tis your estrangéd faces, that miss the many-splendored thing -"

Towards the end of that mini-retreat I prepared in Lent, I spoke of Good Friday (soon to bring Lent to a close). "Good Friday", I suggested, "was for the world's redemption, collectively and individually. Every sorrow we have endured can be lifted with God's Son upon his cross, nothing so appalling that it cannot be - has not been - borne by him. That day of redemptive love, that giving of himself upon the cross, with all its pain, was transformed into the most overwhelming joy on the Sunday of Easter morning."

I should like to read you, either now or perhaps later, an excerpt from a homily for Holy Saturday, written by an ancient anonymous author. It speaks of Christ's rescue of Adam, and by implication the whole human race - and I think you will appreciate how deeply entrenched is the belief in this divine redemption.

What is happening? Today there is a great silence over the earth, a great silence, and stillness, a great silence because the King sleeps; the earth was in terror and was still, because God slept in the flesh and raised up those who were sleeping from the ages. God has died in the flesh, and the underworld has trembled.

Truly he goes to seek out our first parent like a lost sheep; he wishes to visit those who sit in darkness and in the shadow of death. He goes to free the prisoner Adam and his fellow-prisoner Eve from their pains, he who is God, and Adam's son.

The Lord goes in to them holding his victorious weapon, his cross. When Adam, the first created man, sees him, he strikes his breast in terror and calls out to all: 'My Lord be with you all.' And Christ in reply says to Adam: 'And with thy spirit.' And grasping his hand he raises him up saying: 'Awake, O sleeper, and arise from the dead, and Christ shall give you light.

'I am your God, who for your sake became your son, who for you and your descendants now speak and command with authority those in prison: Come forth, and those in darkness: Have light, and those who sleep: Rise.

'I command you: Awake sleeper, I have not made you to be a prisoner in the underworld. Arise from the dead; I am the life of the dead. Arise, O man, work of my hands, arise, you who were fashioned in my image. Rise, let us go hence; for you in me and I in you, together we are one undivided person.

'For you, I your God became your son; for you, I your Master took on your form, that of a slave; for you, I am who am above the heavens came on earth and under the earth; for you, man, I became a man without help, free among the dead; for you, who left a garden, I was handed over to Jews from a garden and crucified in a garden.

'Look at the spittle on my face, which I received because of you, in order to restore you to that first divine inbreathing at creation. See the blows on my cheeks, which I accepted in order to refashion your distorted form to my own image.

'See the scourging on my back, which I accepted in order to dispense the load of your sins which was laid upon your back. See my hands nailed to the tree for a good purpose, for you, who stretched out your hand to the tree for an evil one.

'I slept on the cross and a sword pierced my side, for you, who slept in paradise and brought forth Eve from your side. My side healed the pain of your side; my sleep will release you from your sleep in Hades; my sword has checked the sword which was turned against you.

'But arise, let us go hence. The enemy brought you out of the land of paradise; I will reinstate you, no longer in paradise, but on the throne of heaven. I denied you the tree of life, which was a figure, but now I myself am united to you, I who am life. I posted the cherubim to guard you as they would slaves; now I make the cherubim worship you as they would God.

'The cherubim throne has been prepared, the bearers are ready and waiting, the bridal chamber is in order, the food is provided, the everlasting houses and rooms are in readiness, the treasures of good things have been opened; the kingdom of heaven has been prepared before the ages.'

(From the Second Lesson at Readings for Holy Saturday in the Divine Office)

Sitting beside the dying friend at whose bedside I so recently watched, I thought of this homily.

"You're in for a big surprise, mate!" I assured her unconscious form.

Quiet Day for the Oasis Group
at Duncton Manor

The other day, in a brief interlude of sunlight in this spasmodic summer, I took a friend who was staying with me to the little hamlet in the Downs where I had lived for ten years in a cottage on the Norfolk estate.

Walking up the long chalk lane, the banks recently sheared of their abundant wild flowers, there was, as always, a timeless sense of continuity. One could imagine others down the centuries walking the same path, marvelling at the long view, the river winding through the valley, the distant contours of Arundel Castle silhouetted against the skyline to the south.

This started a train of thought about eternity and the swift passage of our lives in what we glibly describe as 'this world'. How easy it is to become bogged down in the occurrences of each day: the anxieties, the pain of those we love, even the smaller daily trials that seem to taunt us like mosquitoes. Of course these have to be lived through, endured and prayed about, and taking a long view in no way diminishes the effect these circumstances have on our lives, but it struck me as I climbed to the top of that lane how beneficial (for want of a better word) it can be to get 'outside' that little circle of events for a moment.

"Be still and know that I am God" - as the psalmist wrote, demands a quietening of the mind, a conscious opening of the soul which allows God access. As one relaxes, so to speak, it is as if a shaft of recognition illuminates the immensity of God's love, which brings with it a depth of peace that makes itself felt below whatever turmoil might be nearer the surface.

I think we know in our hearts that this 'love' has forever been present (we have been aware of it at special times in our lives) and

I am sure there is a continuity in the life of the soul, the spirit, obscured so often by the circumstances of our busy lives. Have you noticed how the sense of God's presence, of our appreciation of it, often seems to continue as perhaps one door closes and another opens in one's life? It has seemed to me, in the various 'steps in the dark' I have found myself taking, that we bring with us something of what we have learned of God's love into each new situation, a sort of progression or recognition of his gentle leading.

I was re-reading 'The Cloud of Unknowing' recently, and there is a lovely chapter right at the beginning of the book: 'Lift up thine heart unto God,' the author writes, 'with a meek stirring of love; and mean *himself* and none of his goods...This is the work of the soul that most pleaseth God. All saints and angels have joy of this work, and hasten them to help it with all their might. All fiends (devils!) be mad when thou dost thus, and try for to defeat it in all that they can. All men living on earth be wonderfully helped by this work, thou knowest not how. Yea, the souls in purgatory are eased of their pains by virtue of this work. Thou thyself art cleansed and made virtuous by no work so much. And yet it is the lightest work of all, when the soul is helped with grace in sensible desire, and soonest done. Cease not, therefore, but travail therein till thou feel this desire. For at first time that thou dost it, thou findest but a darkness, and as it were a 'cloud of unknowing'... but shape thee and bide in this darkness as long as thou mayest, evermore crying to him whom thou lovest...'

This, of course, is the contemplative way, and not everyone feels drawn to it, but it has this enormous simplicity of intent, so to speak, and its effect is always to increase the awareness of God's love.

In today's world, so often seemingly trivial or increasingly secular, with the horrors and ravages of warfare or disease, I think we can all benefit by that centredness of mind, of an awareness of what (*who*) we have within us. But this awareness has to be practised - which we cannot begin to do unless we have glimpsed the purpose. We read of God's love in the prophet Isaiah, and of the pain he was caused by the disaffection of his chosen. "I spoke to you, and you would not listen, you chose to do what displeases me..." And in the New Testament, even Jesus was driven to admonish the Pharisees, "Jerusalem, Jerusalem, you that kill the prophets and those who are sent to you. How often have I longed to gather your children, as a hen gathers her chicks under her wings, and you refused..."

We tend to forget, I suspect, the 'gathered chicks' because we are in a sort of frenzy of 'requests and beseeching' when we place ourselves before God. (If God cannot perceive our predicaments, then we are, so to speak, barking up the wrong tree!) Of course we pray, but there is also the 'thy will be done' aspect, which sometimes tends to take a back seat in our anxiousness to present our petition. The *Cloud of Unknowing* author encourages us to a deeper perception, but it requires a shutting out for the moment of everything else in order to sense that depth of God's presence. Then we remember Dante: 'In his will is our peace.' I should like to read a passage from *The Cloud*, when he speaks of the *feeling* of God's presence. "But now, mayst thou say: What is this rest (resting in God) that thou speakest of? For methinketh it is travail painful and no rest. For when I set me to do as thou sayest, I find therein no rest, but pain and battle on all sides....To this I answer and say: that thou art not yet used to this work, and therefore it is more painful to thee. But if thou wert wont thereto and knewest by experience what profit were therein, thou wouldst not willingly come out thereof to have all the bodily rest and joy in this world....And therefore go forth with meekness and fervent desire in this work, the which beginneth in this life and never shall have end in the life everlasting. To which I beseech almighty Jesu to bring all those the which he hath bought with his precious blood. Amen"

This whole train of thought was sparked off by the 'long view' we had, as that friend and I walked up the chalk lane in the sunlight. Hardly changed since the mention of it in the Domesday

Book, it was as if history were telescoped, the little church to which on the return way it led, still a witness to the eleventh century, with its two samples of stained. glass - saved from destruction at the reformation. It is a place I greatly love, and last autumn it was rededicated to St Mary the Virgin after restoration by the Conservation of Churches people. Now it can be used for both Anglican and Catholic services at special times during the year. In the meantime, it - and I am sure other special places too - make a perfect setting for the tranquillity of soul we are thinking about. A place where we can catch just a glimpse of the immensity and sureness of God's enduring love for each of us.

'Not what thou art, not what thou hast been, doth God regard with his merciful eyes, but what thou wouldst be...'

Quiet Day for the Oasis Group at Duncton Manor

Great excitement in early May - I had a suspected heart attack and was hastened to Chichester's hospital in an ambulance complete with flashing lights!

After a couple of nights and an angiogram I was allowed home, and the lovely widowed friend who has just come to live next door to me, swept me off to Bailiff's Court at Climping for a luxurious mini-break. The pseudo medieval hotel, complete with peacocks and four-poster beds, was a haven of quiet (despite the peacocks!) We rested and were cosseted in every way, and on the first evening walked the short distance to the sea. The shingle beach was steeply shelved but the receding tide revealed firm wet sand as the gentle waves edged further and further out. We stood there, not needing to speak, watching the movement of the sea, green and grey as the shifting clouds affected the reflection of the sunlight.

There is such a sense of immensity in those elements we take for granted: the sky, the sea, the long horizon. It was relatively calm now, yet one knows how tumultuous a storm can be.

I thought of the terror felt by those disciples of Jesus when the squall came down on the lake and they found the boat taking on water. "Master, master, we are going down -" they cried, and Jesus, asleep in the boat, awoke and rebuked the wind and the rough water, and when they had subsided he said to the disciples "Where is your faith?"

It is strange how 'put to the test' we are by God, almost sometimes as though he were searching out our weakest points! We profess our love for him, our faith and belief in Jesus - and what does he present us with? Difficulties all round.

And yet...I suppose without those stretching times we might remain complacent, possibly a little smug in our cosy beliefs. When I found myself in that cardiac ward, I looked across at "Connie" and "Renie" and "Daph", confined to their beds, elderly and infirm, waiting for their morning tea and pills, and the bright trolley lady, corpulent and cheerful with her "'Mornin' darling", as she took their breakfast orders for "Brown or white, one slice or two?" before the inevitable parade of wheeled-chair commodes and the rattle of bedside curtains.

They, nor I, had expected a stay in hospital, yet there we were, flung together so to speak, almost like shingle on the beach. To change the metaphor, replacing 'people' for 'shingle' how randomly (it sometimes seems) we are washed up together. We, who count ourselves Christian, are primed to see a pattern in this. "Here I am, O Lord, I come to do thy will -" or as that prayer to the Holy Spirit teaches: "Show me what you want me to do and command me to do it -"

One has to abandon oneself to that directing spirit, knowing that this will lead us to a more certain sense of God's presence. Nothing can separate us from him except our forgetting of this fact. He is there even when we are concentrating on tomorrow's lunch, or cleaning our teeth.

Pere de Caussade, the French spiritual writer of the seventeenth century, was noted for his treatise on the abandonment to God's providence. He called it 'the sacrament of the present moment', and I have long found this to be the key to a sense of acceptance when everything appears overbearing. If one takes each moment as coming from (or allowed to come from) God, then there is a measure of peace - albeit sometimes tenuous - in whatever befalls.

And *why* are we subjected to difficulties? We are back to the disciples in the boat again when the storm came up. That must have been great terror. They supposed they would drown. He in whom they had placed all their trust was asleep - *asleep* - and when at last he awoke, having calmed the raging wind and waves, he berated them for their lack of faith. Whose side are we on!

Recently I was at the bedside of someone I had previously known only slightly. Dying of incurable cancer, she had asked me to be with her, but because of my unexpected trip to the cardiac ward it had been impossible to get to her on the morning I had planned. I had to wait a further five days before I could get to the hospice where she had been transferred. I stayed with her only a few minutes, and she asked me to pray that she might soon die. "I'm not afraid," she whispered, "but I wanted you to be here -" She held my hand and together we prayed "into your hands I commend my spirit -" before I placed a sign of the cross on her forehead and tiptoed away. She died a few hours later, very peacefully, her grown-up children beside her. I marvelled again at God's timing, his 'sacrament of the present moment' which Pere de Caussade taught. I had been frustrated in my attempt to visit earlier, but *God* wanted me at that hospice at the particular moment he ordained.

This is such a simple doctrine, and so complete. In the 'abandonment' to God's will we do not merely resign ourselves to his will ("I'm *resigned* to my fate") but we actively *will* what and where he is leading us at a particular moment. When everything appears difficult - by whatever circumstances we find ourselves engulfed - we have to be courageous and let God work in us without ceaseless anxiety, until God's hand does become apparent in whatever currently gives us pain. He isn't in the *pain* but in our *soul*.

Back to the disciples in the sinking boat: Jesus was with them, albeit asleep. What a lesson he taught them! "Where is your FAITH?"

Dom John Chapman, an abbot of Downside many years ago, and a great man of prayer, wrote "You don't need to be 'put right', you *are* all right. If you doubt it, offer yourself to God entirely, and you *are* united to him. There is nothing so simple as the spiritual life. It has no difficulties, no troubles - these are all on the lower, unspiritual part of us. You belong to God. Let that union be your real life, and look down on all the rest. Make light of it, whether it is good or bad, whether it is floods of light, or darkness and devils - it is all God's touch, whether caressing you or hitting you hard...God is everything, and he is all *love* as well as *power*...He is bringing us to himself in his own way, not in our way."

As I prayed with that dying friend, as we said together 'into your hands I commend my spirit' it struck me that it is not only in the great things, the so-to-speak important moments in our lives that we seek him - those are in a way simply landmarks - but in the daily development of our souls, uniquely created to bring us into union with him, to which we abandon ourselves with ever growing devotion.

Quiet Day for the Oasis Group
at Duncton Manor

Tuëma had paintings in an exhibition at Chichester not long ago. It was only a provincial gallery, not one of the important art shows where she exhibits in Dublin or London or Glyndebourne - but as I inspected varied work by local artists, it struck me yet again how diverse are the gifts of the Holy Spirit. Art, literature, music - all stem from inspiration fashioned to our temperament.

I thought of this especially - as I suppose most of us will have done - when we were riveted to the hourly revelations a few weeks ago awaiting those election results. Those unexpected rises and falls, the 'will he or won't he' vacillations culminating in the eventual Morecombe and Wise show in the rose garden of 10 Downing Street. You will, of course, have felt more closely connected or concerned than I, but when the outcome of such national importance hangs in the balance, no one can but be concerned.

"It will never work" we exclaim, as we see opposing parliamentary members seemingly 'coalesced', and "Wait for the first hurdle. I give it a year..." And of course we may be correct, things will not always 'work' according to our presupposed imaginings. But is it not all too easy to rely on our own swift judgement? I think perhaps it is precisely our own judgement that the Holy Spirit comes to overturn!

At Pentecost, when all those apostles were gathered in one room and the 'rushing mighty wind' filled the entire place, the Holy Sprit appeared as tongues of fire. And even as each spoke in different languages, they were understood by those around them. Pretty astonishing! And don't you love those people in Ephesus who, when asked if they had received the Holy Spirit replied

"We never knew there *was* such a thing as the Holy Spirit..."
Subsequently, of course, they went on to be baptised and work in
the local synagogues and so on.

There is a book I read years ago, published in France originally
in 1969. Its title was "*He & I*" and comprised diary entries by a
French woman named Gabriel Bossis. You may have seen it. She
was born in the late nineteenth century, her family were wealthy,
she was attractive and turned down many proposals of marriage,
so that it was assumed she would enter a convent. Yet she felt
impelled to remain 'in the world', writing and producing her own
plays, becoming known throughout France.

Earlier in her life she had been surprised by what she described
as an 'inner voice' which she felt, with awe, to be the voice of
Christ, but it was not until the age of sixty-two that she began
her diaries, which are an almost daily 'dialogue' with him. The
book records these conversations. It begins in 1936 and a lot of the
entries were written whilst travelling in Canada. Her interior voice
(her Voice of Christ) requires her, on January 2nd, to "Offer me
each moment as it passes. This will be enough, because then your
whole year will be for Me..." How simple!

Whenever I have to write retreat notes or perhaps an address
for some occasion, I have long since quoted to myself words I read
from "*He & I*":

"Lend me your hand to write. Lend me your voice to teach the
living truth. Lend me your gestures to love them...Lend me your
kindness. In this way, through you, I shall be among them...Your
influence will be increased and you will think less of yourself. 'This
is not the fruit of my own effort', you will say. 'Jesus was there
with me.' Say it to yourself over and over again; it will keep you
humble. And humility is truth. Lend me your body too, when you
travel, when you toil, when you eat and when you sleep. I did all
these things when I lived among men. Make me live again among
them; and they must be aware of me...I am your centre and your

end. I am your circumference. Wherever your eyes may turn, they will see me. In you, all around you. Everywhere."

Everywhere! Let us not be too worried about coalitions or cutbacks. The Holy Spirit *is* within us, if only we stop for a moment, and listen. He may turn things apparently upside down and make us afraid. But he can also bring new beginnings and surprise us.

I know it is easy to pontificate, and of course we cannot avoid anxiety when long-accepted dependable values seem to falter. I suppose there was never a time when every path was primrose-strewn. In fact we were never promised an *easy* way. We were, however, given the promise of that same Holy Spirit to bring light for our footsteps - and this light need never be limited. Each of us has been given the means to activate the switch.

"Each soul is my favourite," Christ told her, "I choose some only to reach others..."

Quiet Day for the Oasis Group
at Duncton Manor

Judy, next door to me, inherited a Russian icon from her Romanian in-laws. Not large but, like most Russian icons of that era, the actual painting of Christ and his mother was encased in a silver covering of exquisite craftsmanship. Over the course of time the ornate silverwork had somehow become loosened and part of the raised 'halo' had actually broken away. Very gently Judy and I eased the entire silver casing from the wood and there, probably for the first time since it had been painted, we saw the lovely depiction of Mother and Child, slightly out of proportion (as it often will be in Orthodox Christian art) yet executed with minute attention to detail. One could understand the unique vocation, the prayerfulness, demanded of those renowned painters of icons. This one was quite small, but it was not difficult to sense the dedication with which it had been made.

You will see what I am coming to! So much of' what we actually observe is merely the 'silver casing', I feel. What might lie beneath scarcely touches the surface - and it is very easy to jump to conclusions. We read the newspapers, absorb commentaries on this or that and make snap judgements. Even those nearest are not excluded! In a way, we see what we wish to see.

Recently I was called to visit a delightful elderly friend who was dying. He had held a job of responsibility and had retired with honour. But he had smoked all his life and his lungs had succumbed. Even though never practising Christians, his elegant wife thought I might just bestow a measure of comfort. I prayed I might be given the grace to help: 'Lord, keep me out of the way' - is a perennial prayer of mine. When I came into the room where he was propped up in a chair it was a shock to see his deterioration, but his blue eyes still smiled and there was no diminishment of

his humour. "Nice of you to come -" he said with his usual
courtesy. "You know, I do believe in God - but no good becoming
a Roman Catholic - that *would* set the cat amongst the pigeons!"
I laughed, guessing the predicament. I removed the wooden
cross - my Franciscan cross - from where it hung round my neck
and offered this to him. "Would you like that to keep under your
pillow?" I asked. He was glad to take it. "How should I prepare
for dying?" he managed, his breathing difficult. "I think your
best bet is to repeat in your heart 'Into Thy hands I commend my
spirit -' I suggested. "And then lie back, so to speak, and let your
whole being be absorbed into that Love - which is another name
for God -" Then I added "A bit like the dentist's chair in a way!"
knowing the picture would appeal to his sense of the ridiculous.
His cough overcame him and the Macmillan nurse came in to
adjust his morphine. I promised to return soon and I left him, the
little wooden cross in his hand. He died on Maundy Thursday, and
it was a consolation to think he would be part of the Resurrection
on Easter morning.

Had I known Dick much earlier, I should have enjoyed his
companionship and laughter, but I should have been limited by
the exterior personality - as each of us is by what we observe
on the surface. Why does it seem to take pain or great love to reach
the inner kernel? We are back to Holy Week and the Crucifixion,
and the whole magnificence of Easter...

I re-read Archbishop Anthony Bloom's 'School for Prayer' the
other day and should love to quote you what he wrote on the
subject of daily prayer. I found it rang so true.

'Awake in the morning', he wrote, 'and the first thing you do,
thank God for it, even if you don't feel particularly happy about
the day which is to come. "This day was made by the Lord, let us
rejoice and be glad in it." Once you have done this, give yourself
time to realise what you are saying and really mean it - perhaps
on the level of deep conviction and not of what one might call
exhilaration. And then get up, wash, clean do whatever else you

have to do, and then come to God again. Come to God again with two convictions. The one is that you are God's own, and the other is that this day is also God's own, it is absolutely new, absolutely fresh. It has never existed before. To speak in Russian terms, it is like a vast expanse of untrodden snow. No one has trodden on it yet. It is all virgin and pure in front of you. What comes next is that you ask God to bless this day, that everything in it should be blessed and ruled by Him. After that you must take it seriously, because very often one says "O God bless me", and having got the blessing we act like the prodigal son - we collect all our goods and go to a strange country and lead a riotous life.

'This day is blessed by God, it is God's own and now let us go into it. You walk in this day as God's own messenger; whoever you meet, you must meet in God's own way. You are there to be the presence of the Lord God, the presence of Christ, the presence of the Spirit, the presence of the Gospel - this is your function on this particular day. God has never said that when you walk into a situation in His own name that He will be crucified and you will be the risen one. You must be prepared to walk into situations, one after the other in God's name, to walk as the Son of God has done: in humiliation and humility, in truth and ready to be persecuted and so on. Usually what we expect when we fulfil God's commandments is to see a marvellous result at once - we read of that at times in the lives of the saints. When, for instance, someone hits us on one cheek, we turn the other one, although we don't expect to be hit at all, but we expect to hear the other person say "What humility -" you get your reward and he gets the salvation of his soul. It does not work that way. You must pay the cost and very often you get hit hard. What matters is that you are prepared for that. As to the day, if you accept that this day was blessed of God, chosen by God of His own hand, then every person you meet is a gift of God, every circumstance you meet is a gift of God, whether it is bitter or sweet, whether you like or dislike it.'

Every person you meet is a gift of God...and that 'gift' applies to the window cleaner, the postman or indeed your very nearest and dearest...As the Duchess of Cambridge so graphically exclaimed as she stepped on to the balcony at Buckingham Palace, "*Wow!*" You have the whole world before you! All God's gift!

We may be despondent or dazzled - or simply distracted by the ornate silverwork encasing what is hidden, but once we perceive that a precious soul lies just below the surface, we have access to a gift more priceless than the costliest icon in the world. As the poet Francis Thompson wrote in that lovely poem '*In No Strange Land*':

> The angels keep their ancient places -
> Turn but a stone and start a wing!
> 'Tis ye, 'tis your estranged faces,
> That miss the many-splendored thing.

Quiet Day for the Oasis Group
at Duncton Manor

I am writing this with a blustery wind and frequent showers playing havoc with the garden, and no sign of a let up. Lent with its hardships has gone, Easter too, and that amazing Diamond Jubilee, holding us spellbound, took place only last weekend. By the time we meet in July we shall he stiffening our sinews for the Olympic Games...

A long known friend, Peter Richey, came to see me the other day. He lives on his own in the house his grandmother left him, perched on a cliff above Lee Bay in North Devon. Years ago, he and his brother Simon wrote a song called 'Occasional Rain' which was taken up by Cliff Richard, and they still receive small royalties from re-issues. Now in his sixties, he has always kept in touch. He was a cousin of the friend I'd hoped to work with when I obtained my leave from the convent. It was from his boat that I scattered Elizabeth's ashes when she succumbed to her untimely cancer.

Peter and I ate lunch in the cottage here, reminiscing easily about family and recalling our younger days. He told me how he had always loved music. I read him some of my very youthful verse. We rather enjoyed the comparisons of our natural development over the years.

Thinking of this, it struck me that of course every one of us has this individual 'seed' within. Never identical, but there to be nurtured. "What", I thought, "is the source of this nurturing?" The ancient fathers of the Church tell us that *grace* builds on nature. By grace, they mean the Spirit of Christ, the Holy Spirit, which is bestowed on us at Whitsun, Pentecost, and there for us to call upon, to recognise, and to turn to in all our needs. As that 'seed' of our individual being develops, we become the people we are, and we learn to choose. I remember being taught at my prep school the verse from Philippians chapter 4 verse 13: St Paul writes 'I can do all things through Christ which strengtheneth me.' 'Christ which strengtheneth me' is not some ephemeral wisp. He is truly *there*. Sometimes I don't think we really understand this until something totally rocks our boats: an illness of our own, perhaps, or the unspeakable loss of someone dear. Suddenly our way of life, our faith, seems reduced to a heap of ashes. Like the disciples caught in the storm we want to yell "*Save us*, Lord, or we sink -" (yet in our agony we probably cannot think of the Lord at all. We are alone in our despair.)

Back to the seed within. Still there beneath the pain, the agony, the wretchedness...and it may take a long time before we are able to discern any sort of glimmer. And then one day, there may come a sense that somehow you are free - free in your spirit. What you had thought of as shackling, you will discover is a sort of liberation. The pain becomes, as it were, a 'transformed' pain. Perhaps we might even look back on that agony as almost a form of fertiliser for our inner seed. I remember reading a book by William Johnston called '*Being in Love, a Practice of Christian Prayer*' and I copied a paragraph that particularly struck me.

'When with tears and anguish and pain you have said goodbye to everything, you will find that you have lost nothing. You have said goodbye only to the clinging and attachment of things..."All things are yours, and you are Christ's and Christ is God's" You will gradually come to an inner freedom. You can become one with the poor, the sick and the suffering...And you can love... You may find you can love your friends not for the security they give you, but for what they are in themselves. You may find that you love everyone you meet in the street or on the bus. And you will experience a wonderful flowering of your personality, as unexplored and untapped potential rises to the surface of your consciousness. Other talents come to the fore - talents you never dreamed you possessed. You have become a richer person.'

So you can see, I think, what I meant when I referred to the conversation I had with Peter Richey. Through vicissitudes, through the twists and unforeseen circumstances of our lives, this uniquely individual seed does develop, does come, by God's grace, to fruition. "Without Him," says St Paul again, "I can do nothing - but I can do all things through Christ...-"

Peter's song, 'Occasional Rain', written with Simon in the sixties, included the lines:

'Occasional rain will teach us
Never to rely
On a bright blue sky -
Always be prepared for grey -'

We are older now, but we relate to that youthful observation! Our own 'bright blue sky' today, depends on no weather forecast, but on the certainty of that love within us, which is the fruit of God's gift to us. We may become artists, or musicians, or parents or grandparents, mathematicians or gardeners - the scope is as wide as God's creation. In everything we shall come to see that it was He who planted the seed, and it is in Him that we live and move and have our being.

Quiet Day for the Oasis Group in London

I've been watching the peregrine falcon chicks hatched behind the crenellated base of Chichester Cathedral spire. The falcons return each year and are a constant focus for innumerable 'twitchers', cameras trained, and even a television link so that the comings and goings can be viewed incessantly. They can be a huge and delightful time waster!

And you can see how my mind turned to St Matthew, where Jesus admonishes Jerusalem: 'How often have I longed to gather your children as a hen gathers her chicks under her wings, and you refused...'

It is so easy to imagine one can travel unaided. We cherish our independence - yet our independence can, I suspect, sometimes be a sort of - well - pride perhaps? And there is Jesus, beckoning us to enlist his help, his guidance, and we make the excuse that we do not wish to be a burden, as if we were a sack of potatoes, let alone a chick.

Isn't that the wonderful thing about Christ's love for us? He *longs* for us to acknowledge our dependence on him. Re-reading my beloved Julian of Norwich, in the first Revelation of Divine Love, she tells us: 'He is for clothing that for love wrappeth us, claspeth us, and all encloseth us for tender love, that he may never leave us.' We find it difficult to get our heads round this - as if the sense of his presence had to be tangible in the way we experience a beloved human presence. Yet that is what he promised, and sometimes it takes pain or deprivation to realise that, within the pain, perhaps beyond the external senses, Jesus *is* there, a flame kindled within our deepest being. He is within our *soul*.

And I suppose what we have to aim at is the acceptance of the *fact* of his presence, and to train ourselves to look within, where he dwells: a sort of inextinguishable candle, and a light to guide our path.

Back to the chicks again: it is warm beneath those sheltering wings, and once we have found that sanctuary within, we must try never to let anxiety or fear overcome us as we face the unexperienced demands of our lives. I have noticed there comes a sort of physical deprivation as we become older - I hate having to depend on a stick - and I long to dig the weed-infested garden and am much inhibited when prevented. Each of us has limitations, they are part of life's pattern, whatever our age or circumstance - a sort of red traffic light to frustrate our progress - yet this is where me must learn to find him.

"Help, help and rescue! Piglet cried", we remember from A. A. Milne when we were six - and "All shall be well" echoes Julian of Norwich from a much earlier date, "and all manner of things shall be well"...

Easily spoken or read from a tastefully printed book-mark - but we must learn to *live* that directive from Jesus: 'All shall be well' implies that all *is* well. Just as it is for those protected chicks, safely enfolded on my cathedral spire.

Nothing, nothing at all, can separate us from the love of Christ.

Mini-address for the Oasis Group

When I told friends that I was planning to leave the rather spacious flat I rented in the Close at Chichester, there was a lot of apprehension. I made the move at the end of July and am, after weeks of workmen and vicissitudes, now established in a dear little house in Petersfield, and feel as if I had never been anywhere else. I had friends there anyway, and through them was able to contact various handymen whom I employed to replace rotted trellis or hack down greatly overgrown shrubs inextricably entwined in the garden.

Which brings me to the small, and sometimes I think relevant, point I wanted to share with you today: *pruning*. Cutting things back, metaphorically using the secateurs, cultivating the tender shoots and being tough with those insidious roots like ground elder. (Once, incidentally, when I was trying to make a garden behind the adorable cottage at North Stoke, I was so maddened by the ground elder that I isolated it in a bed of its own. People would stop to admire it, enquiring what it was!)

You can see the analogy, and the way my thought is going. "Cuts" in life *hurt*. We each will have had them, some a great deal more painful than anything secateurs can do. There are some incisions where the scars are ineradicable. I am thinking now of less life-changing pain, more of those aggravations which, like midges or mosquitoes, beset our daily plans or routine. They make us lash out, swatting unsuccessfully with metaphoric rolled-up newspapers, or resulting in complaint or envy - much more contagious - comparing our irritations with what we mistakenly assume the tranquil environment of our acquaintance.

One bright afternoon in October, I decided to tackle the raised bed bordering my front windows. Being unsteady on my feet,

I climbed on to the bed with the help of my stick, exchanging it for the spade which I'd propped against the wall. I then tried to follow the plan I had devised for the roses. (It is astonishing what one can achieve with the help of one's guardian angel, to whom I am totally indebted!) I planted five rose bushes, incorporating bone meal and rose food - bags of compost and farmyard manure had been forked in by my original handyman - and interspersed them with small shrubs, like species lilac and, at the back, that scented shrub whose name I cannot spell, to waft across the driveway from November onwards. One day I hope to secrete a small bench beneath the climbing New Dawn, so that I can catch the sun, my whereabouts shielded from view to the uninitiated!

It is so tempting never to prune in one's life. We cannot be bothered to attend to those straggly bits. I'm not advocating a Franciscan vow of poverty - I simply feel that it is so easy to become 'sloppy' about ourselves. Maybe our point of view, or our attachment out of a sort of lethargy, to attitudes we cannot be bothered to change. Sometimes, I think, it takes the daily newspaper, or the news from our television, to bring us up suddenly to an appalling situation that simply had not occurred to us.

It just struck me, as I struggled with that small flower bed, so recently entangled with innumerable run-to-seed berberis, holly bushes and indistinguishable weeds, that our own lives, like gardens, could so well benefit from a sort of 'clipping back' from time to time. There might even be the opportunity for a spot of mulch or good old stable manure.

I thought Advent might be quite a good time to think about that. And the results next year could be spectacular.

LOVE
(from Thomas Traherne 1637 – 1674)

Love is so divine and perfect a thing that it is worthy to be the very end and being of the Deity. It is His goodness and it is His glory. We therefore so vastly delight in love of all these excellencies and all whatsoever lie within it. By loving a soul does propagate and magnify itself. By loving it does enlarge and delight itself. By loving it also delighteth others, and by loving it doth honour and enrich itself. Love also being the end of souls which are never perfect till they are in act what they are in power. They were made to love and are dark and vain and comfortless until they do it. Till they love, they are idle or misemployed. Till they love, they are desolate without their objects, and narrow and little. But when they shine by love upon all objects, they are accompanied with them and enlightened by them. Till we become, therefore all act as God is, we can never rest nor ever be satisfied.

Love is so noble that it enjoyeth others' enjoyments, delighting in giving all unto its object. So that whosoever loveth all mankind, he enjoyeth all the goodness of God and the whole world, and endeavoureth the benefit of kingdoms and ages, with all whom he is present by love, which is the best manner of presence that is possible.

God is present by love alone. By love also He is great and glorious. By love alone He liveth and feeleth in other persons, By Love alone He enjoyeth all creatures, by love alone He is pleasing to Himself, by love alone He is rich and blessed.

O why dost thou not by love alone seek to achieve all these, by love alone attain thy glory? The same is shrivelled up and buried in a grave that does not love. But that which does love wisely and truly is joy and end of all the world, the King of Heaven, and the friend of God, the shining light and temple of eternity, the brother of Christ Jesus, and one spirit with the Holy Ghost.